GOURMET
AUSTRALIAN
menus

Editor Kathy Snowball
Art director Hieu Nguyen
Copy editor Anna Macdonald
Wine consultant Peter Bourne
Menu introductions Meg Thomason
Proofreading Julie Collard

Chief executive officer John Alexander
Group publisher Jill Baker
Publisher Sue Wannan

Produced by ACP Books.
Colour separations by ACP Colour Graphics Pty Ltd, Sydney.
Printed by Toppan Printing, Hong Kong.
Published by ACP Publishing Pty Limited, 54 Park Street, Sydney, NSW 2001 (GPO Box 4088, Sydney, NSW 1028),
phone (02) 9282 8618, fax (02) 9267 9438, awwhomelib@acp.com.au www.awwbooks.com.au
AUSTRALIA: Distributed by Network Distribution Company, GPO Box 4088, Sydney, NSW 1028,
phone (02) 9282 8777, fax (02) 9264 3278.
UNITED KINGDOM: Distributed by Australian Consolidated Press (UK), Moulton Park Business Centre, Red House Road,
Moulton Park, Northampton, NN3 6AQ, phone (01604) 497 531, fax (01604) 497 533, acpukltd@aol.com
CANADA: Distributed by Whitecap Books Ltd, 351 Lynn Avenue, North Vancouver, BC, V7J 2C4, phone (604) 980 9852.
NEW ZEALAND: Distributed by Netlink Distribution Company, Level 4, 23 Hargreaves Street, College Hill,
Auckland 1, phone (9) 302 7616.
SOUTH AFRICA: Distributed by PSD Promotions (Pty) Ltd, PO Box 1175, Isando 1600, SA, phone (011) 392 6065,
and CNA Limited, Newsstand Division, PO Box 10799, Johannesburg 2000, SA, phone (011) 491 7500.

Gourmet menus.

Includes index.
ISBN 1 86396 251 4.

1. Food. 2. Cookery. I. Title: Australian Women's Weekly.

641.514

Front cover: Poached honey pears with ricotta. Styling by Sophia Young. Photography by Ian Wallace.
Back cover: Styling by Sophia Young. Photography by George Seper.

GOURMET
AUSTRALIAN

menus
ACP PUBLISHING

foreword

Here is a treasury of meals with the *Australian Gourmet Traveller* hallmark – beautiful and interesting yet unfussed and workable for real life. This book covers all occasions, from fast and simple weeknight meals to dinner parties, cocktail parties, picnics and barbecues – more than 100 of the best recipes from the pages of *Australian Gourmet Traveller* magazine, plus many more that have never been published. For further inspiration, extra menu suggestions, compiled from the recipes in the book, are listed at the back, where you will also find a section of recipes for such basics as stocks, sauces and so on. For each menu – apart from the two-page menus which are called simple and are just that, designed to come together easily – we've given a time plan suggesting how to organise your day and what can be prepared in advance. You'll also find wine suggestions for each menu, but don't worry if you can't find the wine mentioned – simply choose a similar wine style and grape variety. This book is dedicated to all the cooks who love our recipes and have been wanting us to collect them in a compact form for easy reference. We hope you will enjoy cooking from these menus.

contents

menus for warm weather

menus for cool weather

menus for warm weather

asian picnic

menu serves 12

prawns and scallops with kaffir-lime leaves and ponzu

barbecued duck and beetroot rice-paper rolls

ocean trout and noodle salad

chinese five-spice pork with charred baby corn

pan-fried green-onion and chilli bread

coconut and passionfruit tart

lemon vodka cocktails

time planner

one day ahead: keep covered in refrigerator

- make ponzu
- shred duck and combine with hoisin-sauce mixture
- prepare vegetables for rice-paper rolls
- cook ocean trout
- marinate and roast pork, char-grill corn
- bake coconut tart
- make lemon syrup for cocktails

on the day

- thread prawns and scallops onto skewers
and barbecue
- assemble rice-paper rolls
- prepare noodles and dressing and combine
with flaked trout
- cook bread
- make lemon vodka cocktails
- assemble all dishes, transport to picnic and serve

PRAWNS AND SCALLOPS WITH KAFFIR-LIME LEAVES AND PONZU

23 kaffir-lime leaves
20 large scallops, roe removed
20 large uncooked prawns, peeled
    and deveined, leaving tails intact
20 x 15cm bamboo skewers,
    soaked in hot water for 10 minutes
$1/4$ cup sesame oil
2 teaspoons roasted
    black and white sesame seeds

PONZU

2 tablespoons lemon juice
2 tablespoons soy sauce
2 tablespoons mirin

Very finely shred 3 of the smallest kaffir-lime leaves. Thread a scallop, a lime leaf and a prawn onto each bamboo skewer and place in a glass or ceramic baking dish. Brush skewers with a little sesame oil, sprinkle with shredded kaffir-lime leaf and season to taste. Char-grill or barbecue skewers until seafood is just tender.

For ponzu, combine all ingredients and mix well.

Serve skewers sprinkled with sesame seeds and pass ponzu for dipping.

Makes 20.

Asian food translates very well to a picnic with style. Nearly everything here can be eaten with the fingers, while the one exception, the salad, is neatly served in nifty little containers.

PRAWNS AND SCALLOPS WITH KAFFIR-LIME LEAVES AND PONZU

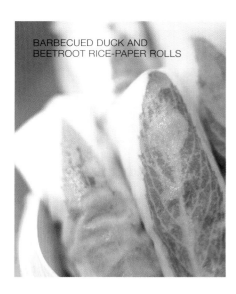

BARBECUED DUCK AND
BEETROOT RICE-PAPER ROLLS

BARBECUED DUCK AND BEETROOT RICE-PAPER ROLLS

1/3 cup hoisin sauce
1 tablespoon mirin
1 fresh, small red chilli,
   seeded and finely chopped
1 tablespoon sesame oil
1 barbecued chinese duck
20 x 20cm rice-paper rounds
20 mint leaves
2 lebanese cucumbers,
   halved lengthwise, seeded
   and cut into 6-7cm lengths
12 green onions, trimmed
   to 6cm and cut into strips
1 large cooked beetroot (about 275g),
   peeled and cut into 6cm batons
240g (3 cups) beansprouts
20 small sprigs of coriander

Combine hoisin sauce, mirin, chilli and sesame oil in a bowl and mix well.

Remove meat and skin from duck and discard fatty bits. Shred duck meat and skin very thinly, then combine with hoisin-sauce mixture.

Soak rice papers in hot water, in batches, until just softened, then place on damp tea towels, covering with another damp tea towel as you work. Place a mint leaf widthwise on a softened rice paper, 3cm from the bottom, then top with some cucumber, green onion, beetroot, duck mixture, beansprouts and a coriander sprig. Fold over bottom edge of rice paper, then fold in sides and roll up like a spring roll. Repeat with remaining rice-paper rounds and ingredients. Place rice-paper rolls on plastic-wrap-lined trays, cover with damp absorbent paper, then cover trays with plastic wrap and refrigerate until needed.

Makes 20.

OCEAN TROUT AND NOODLE SALAD

3 ocean trout fillets (about 200g each),
   skinned and pin-boned
250g green mung-bean noodles
Grated rind of 1 lime
1/2 cup lime juice
1/4 cup fish sauce
50g dark palm sugar, grated
1 stick of lemongrass,
   white part only, finely chopped
1 fresh, small red chilli,
   seeded and finely chopped
1 tablespoon peanut oil
1 bunch of radishes (about 500g),
   trimmed and very thinly sliced
300g peas, podded to give 120g,
   blanched in boiling water
   for 3 minutes, then drained
   and refreshed in cold water
1/4 cup drained pickled ginger
6 green onions, sliced on the diagonal
1 cup coriander leaves
1/2 cup mint leaves, torn

Bring 2cm of water to the boil in a large saucepan, add ocean trout, cover with a tight-fitting lid and poach over low heat for 3 minutes. Turn heat off and cool trout in covered pan. When cool, remove trout from water and flake into large pieces.

Place noodles in a bowl, cover with plenty of warm water and soak for 15 minutes or until softened, then drain.

Combine lime rind and juice, fish sauce, palm sugar, lemongrass, chilli and peanut oil in a bowl and stir until sugar dissolves.

Combine noodles and remaining ingredients, except ocean trout, in a bowl and toss gently. Add dressing and flaked ocean trout and toss gently until combined.

CHINESE FIVE-SPICE PORK WITH CHARRED BABY CORN

1 large tomato, coarsely chopped
2 tablespoons tomato paste
2 fresh, small red chillies,
    seeded and coarsely chopped
3 teaspoons ground star anise
3 teaspoons ground cinnamon
1 teaspoon ground fennel seed
1/4 teaspoon ground cloves
1 x 4cm piece of ginger, grated
6 cloves of garlic
1 1/2 tablespoons fish sauce
100g (1/2 cup, firmly packed)
    brown sugar
1/4 cup soy sauce
1 x 2kg boneless pork belly,
    rind removed and fat trimmed to 3mm
Plum sauce, to serve

CHARRED BABY CORN
230g baby corn
1/4 cup sesame oil

Process all ingredients, except pork, in a food processor until a paste forms. Place pork in a glass or ceramic dish, add paste and turn pork to coat, then cover and refrigerate for 1 hour.

Line a roasting pan with foil and fit with a greased roasting rack or wire rack. Remove pork from marinade (reserve marinade) and place, fat side down, on wire rack in pan and roast at 180C for 30 minutes, turn, then brush with a little reserved marinade and cook for 1 hour, basting every 15 minutes. Cook for another 30 minutes, without basting, until top is dark and crisp. Cool.

For charred baby corn, combine corn and sesame oil, season to taste and mix well. Char-grill or barbecue corn until lightly charred and just cooked.

Serve sliced pork with plum sauce, charred baby corn and pan-fried green-onion and chilli bread (recipe follows).

PAN-FRIED GREEN-ONION AND CHILLI BREAD

20 green onions, thinly sliced
1 cup coriander leaves
1/2 cup garlic chives, finely chopped
600g (4 cups) plain flour
1 tablespoon baking powder
2 teaspoons salt
2 tablespoons sesame oil
1 tablespoon chilli oil
Peanut oil, for shallow-frying

Combine green onion, coriander and chive and set aside. Process sifted flour, baking powder and salt in a food processor. Using the pulse button, add combined oils and 1 1/3 cups warm water and pulse until mixture just comes together. Cover and refrigerate for 15 minutes. Divide dough in half, roll each portion into a 36cm log and cut each log into 12 pieces, then place pieces, cut side down, on a board (cover pieces with plastic wrap until ready to use). Roll pieces, in batches, on a lightly floured surface until 15cm round and top with green-onion mixture. Press onion mixture lightly into dough and roll up like a swiss roll, then form roll into a spiral. Flatten spiral and roll out until 12cm round.

Add 3mm peanut oil to a heavy-based frying pan and pan-fry bread, in batches, over medium heat for 1-2 minutes on each side until golden, adding more oil as necessary.

Makes 24.

CHINESE FIVE-SPICE PORK WITH
CHARRED BABY CORN; PAN-FRIED
GREEN-ONION AND CHILLI BREAD

LEMON VODKA COCKTAILS

COCONUT AND PASSIONFRUIT TART

180g plain flour
30g icing sugar
110g cold unsalted butter, chopped
1 egg

FILLING

2 eggs
200g caster sugar
1/2 cup strained passionfruit juice
    (about 8 passionfruit)
1 teaspoon grated orange rind
1 1/2 cups pouring cream
250g desiccated coconut

Process flour, icing sugar, a pinch of salt and butter in a food processor until mixture resembles fine breadcrumbs, add egg and process until mixture just comes together. Form dough into a disc, wrap in plastic wrap and refrigerate for 30 minutes. Roll out dough on a lightly floured surface until 3mm thick and line a round 28cm flan tin with removable base with pastry. Cover and freeze for 1 hour. Line pastry with baking paper, fill with dried beans or rice and bake at 190C for 10 minutes. Remove paper and beans and bake for another 10 minutes or until pastry is golden and dry. Cool.

For filling, beat eggs and caster sugar until pale and smooth. Add passionfruit juice and orange rind and whisk until just combined, then add cream and coconut and whisk until just combined. Spoon filling into pastry case and bake at 180C for 35-40 minutes or until just set and lightly browned. Cool. Refrigerate overnight before serving in wedges.

LEMON VODKA COCKTAILS

12 mint leaves
160g caster sugar
100ml lemon juice
250ml vodka
Lemon wedges, to serve

Tie mint leaves together with a small piece of string. Combine caster sugar and 300ml water in a small saucepan and stir over medium heat until sugar dissolves and mixture boils. Remove from heat, add mint leaves and cool to room temperature. Remove mint leaves and refrigerate syrup until cold, then combine with lemon juice and vodka and mix well. Pour lemon vodka cocktails into glasses with plenty of ice and serve with lemon wedges.

wines: Here are some suggestions for what to drink with these dishes. **Coopers Original Pale Ale, SA.** Due to its extended yeast lees contact, this is a full-flavoured style, the perfect "food" beer. **Ashbrook Estate Verdelho, Margaret River, WA.** This classy verdelho shows loads of typical pineapple and passionfruit flavours with an edge of regional herbaceousness. Verdelho's upfront flavours and zesty acidity make it a perfect picnic white. **Wyndham Estate Bin 888 Cabernet Merlot, Hunter Valley, NSW.** Cabernet sauvignon can be quite firm in its youth, whereas merlot is a soft and generous variety from the outset. This marriage of cabernet and merlot is rich enough to tame the hoisin sauce and soft enough to go with the spiced pork.

COCONUT AND PASSIONFRUIT TART

simple light lunch

menu serves 6

grilled pear, mozzarella and prosciutto salad

poached snapper with shaved asparagus and tomato and fennel-seed salad

summer compote of watermelon and blackberries

GRILLED PEAR, MOZZARELLA AND PROSCIUTTO SALAD

3 small pears, quartered,
    cored and cut into eighths
Olive oil
12 slices of prosciutto
200g baby rocket leaves
3 buffalo mozzarella, thinly sliced
2 tablespoons lemon juice
30g (1/4 cup) roasted walnuts, crumbled

Brush pear slices with olive oil and char-grill on both sides over high heat until browned. Place prosciutto on a wire rack over an oven tray and roast at 200C for 5-10 minutes or until crisp.

Place rocket on 6 plates and top with pear and mozzarella. Drizzle with combined lemon juice and 2 tablespoons olive oil and sprinkle with walnuts and cracked black pepper. Top each with 2 slices of prosciutto.

wine: Peter Lehmann Semillon, Barossa Valley, SA.

POACHED SNAPPER WITH SHAVED ASPARAGUS AND TOMATO AND FENNEL-SEED SALAD

6 egg tomatoes, quartered,
    then halved crosswise
Extra virgin olive oil
1 teaspoon roasted fennel seeds,
    lightly crushed
1/4 cup lemon juice
1/2 cup flat-leaf parsley leaves
2 tablespoons white-wine vinegar
6 snapper fillets (about 200g each),
    skin on, halved crosswise
3 bunches of asparagus, trimmed

Place tomato on an oven tray, drizzle with a little extra virgin olive oil and roast at 100C for 1 hour. Cool, then toss with fennel, lemon juice and parsley.

Fill 2 large frying pans with water, divide vinegar between pans and bring to the boil. Add snapper fillets to each pan, turn off heat and stand for 7-10 minutes or until snapper is just cooked.

Meanwhile, cut off asparagus tips and place in the top of a steamer. Using a vegetable peeler, shave remaining asparagus into strips and place on top of tips. Season with sea salt and steam over simmering water until just heated through.

Place asparagus on 6 plates, top each with 2 pieces of fish and tomato and fennel-seed salad and drizzle plates with a little extra virgin olive oil.

wine: Tyrrell's She-Oak Unwooded Chardonnay, Hunter Valley, NSW.

SUMMER COMPOTE OF WATERMELON AND BLACKBERRIES

50g caster sugar
1 vanilla bean, split lengthwise
500ml light pinot noir or grenache
1kg watermelon, rind removed
500g ripe blackberries

Combine sugar, scraped seeds of vanilla bean, the vanilla bean and half the wine in a small saucepan and stir over medium heat until sugar dissolves, then bring to the boil and simmer for 3 minutes. Cool.

Cut watermelon into small wedges. Combine watermelon and blackberries in a large bowl with the cooled syrup and remaining wine. Mix gently, then cover and refrigerate for 1 hour before serving.

wine: Brown Brothers Moscato, Milawa, Vic.

Eating lightly needn't mean giving up
luxurious tastes and textures. This low-fat
dinner is special by any standard.

vegetarian lunch party

WARM OLIVES WITH EGGPLANT DIP

MIXED VEGETABLE PLATE WITH
SHEEP'S-MILK YOGHURT DRESSING

WARM OLIVES WITH EGGPLANT DIP

2 large eggplant (about 400g each)
8 cloves of garlic, skin on
Extra virgin olive oil
1/4 cup Greek-style plain yoghurt
2 tablespoons tahini
1/4 cup lemon juice
2 tablespoons finely chopped
    flat-leaf parsley
1 fresh, small red chilli,
    seeded and finely chopped
200g large kalamata olives
Sliced toasted turkish bread, to serve

Pierce eggplant all over with a fork and place with garlic in a roasting pan, drizzle with a little olive oil and roast at 200C for 40 minutes or until eggplant and garlic are very soft. When eggplant is cool enough to handle, remove skin, chop flesh coarsely and drain in a colander for 10 minutes. Process drained eggplant and peeled garlic in a food processor until coarsely chopped. Add 1/4 cup extra virgin olive oil, yoghurt, tahini, lemon juice, parsley and chilli and process until smooth, then season to taste.

Just before serving, place olives in a small roasting pan, drizzle with a little extra virgin olive oil and heat in oven at 190C for 10-15 minutes or until warmed through. Spoon olives and eggplant dip into separate bowls and place on a plate with slices of toasted turkish bread.

Eggplant dip makes about 2 cups.

time planner

one day ahead: keep covered in refrigerator

• make eggplant dip

• prepare sheep's-milk yoghurt dressing

• bake tart shells: keep in airtight container

on the day

• roast vegetables and barbecue mushrooms

• prepare pea purée

• prepare butter mixture
and peel and stuff peaches

• roast olives and toast turkish bread
and serve with eggplant dip

• serve vegetable plate and yoghurt dressing

• deep-fry cauliflower, assemble tarts,
make radicchio salad and serve

• roast peaches, add raspberries and serve

Revelling in vegetables – smoothed into
a piquant dip, paired with crisp pastry
or fresh in a salad. Even non-vegetarians
will love to share this feast.

ROASTED PEACHES AND RASPBERRIES
IN ALMOND-LIQUEUR SYRUP

LITTLE PEA AND CAULIFLOWER
TARTS WITH RADICCHIO SALAD

MIXED VEGETABLE PLATE WITH SHEEP'S-MILK YOGHURT DRESSING

1 bunch of dutch carrots,
   peeled and tops trimmed to 1cm
1 1/2 teaspoons cumin seeds
2 cloves of garlic, thinly sliced
Olive oil
8 baby beetroot (about 500g),
   stalks trimmed to 2cm
2 corella pears, quartered and cored
1 1/2 tablespoons balsamic vinegar
Walnut oil
8 large field mushrooms,
   peeled and stalks trimmed

SHEEP'S-MILK YOGHURT DRESSING

200g sheep's-milk yoghurt
2 tablespoons sour cream
2 teaspoons lemon juice
1 tablespoon chopped coriander

For sheep's-milk yoghurt dressing, combine all ingredients with 1 tablespoon water, mix well, then season to taste.

Combine carrots, cumin and garlic in a small roasting pan, season to taste and drizzle with a little olive oil. Wrap beetroot together in foil and place to one side in a roasting pan. Place beetroot on top shelf in oven and carrots on lower shelf and roast at 200C for 20 minutes. Place pear in the same pan as beetroot, season to taste and drizzle with balsamic vinegar and a little olive oil, then return to oven and bake for another 15 minutes or until vegetables and pear are tender. Remove beetroot from foil, peel away skins and drizzle with a little walnut oil.

Brush mushrooms generously with olive oil and season to taste. Char-grill or barbecue until just tender.

Place vegetables and pear warm or at room temperature on 8 plates and pass sheep's-milk yoghurt dressing separately.

wine: Brokenwood Semillon, Hunter Valley, NSW. Semillon is one of the best food whites, especially for more savoury food flavours, such as the vegetables, olives and eggplant in these appetisers. Semillon's high natural acidity will work well with the zing of the yoghurt dressing.

LITTLE PEA AND CAULIFLOWER TARTS WITH RADICCHIO SALAD

225g (1 1/2 cups) plain flour
180g cream cheese, chopped
1 egg
4 baby cauliflower, halved
2 egg whites, lightly whisked
Cornflour seasoned to taste, for dusting
Vegetable oil, for deep-frying

PEA FILLING

1.5kg peas, podded to give 600g
2 shallots, coarsely chopped
2 tablespoons mint leaves
80g butter, chopped
1/2 cup pouring cream

RADICCHIO SALAD

1 head of radicchio, trimmed
   and leaves separated
1/2 cup torn mint leaves
1 tablespoon walnut oil
2 1/2 tablespoons white-wine vinegar

Process flour and cream cheese in a food processor until mixture resembles coarse breadcrumbs, add egg and process until mixture just comes together. Divide dough into 8 discs, wrap in plastic wrap and refrigerate for 30 minutes. Roll out each pastry disc until 3mm thick and line 8 round 10cm (3cm-deep) tart tins, with removable bases. Prick pastry bases with a fork, then freeze for 1 hour. Line pastry cases with baking paper and fill with rice or dried beans, place on an oven tray and bake blind at 190C for 10 minutes, then remove paper and beans and bake for 10 minutes or until dry and crisp. Cool.

For pea filling, add peas, shallot and mint to a saucepan of boiling, salted water and cook for 5-8 minutes or until peas are just tender. Drain and process hot pea mixture with remaining ingredients in a food processor until smooth, then season to taste. Push pea mixture through a fine sieve, then return to saucepan, cover and stand in a warm place.

Toss cauliflower halves in egg white, then into seasoned cornflour and shake away excess. Deep-fry cauliflower immediately, in batches, in hot vegetable oil until crisp and lightly browned, then drain on absorbent paper.

For radicchio salad, combine radicchio and mint in a bowl, add walnut oil and vinegar, season to taste and toss gently to combine.

Divide salad among 8 plates. Spoon pea filling into tart shells, top with a cauliflower half and serve beside salad.

wine: Bushranger Bounty Chardonnay, Cowra, NSW. Chardonnay offers the widest range of both weight and flavours of any white variety. This newcomer from Cowra is lightly oaked and not too high in alcohol, yet it has sufficient acidity to maintain a fresh and zesty finish.

ROASTED PEACHES AND RASPBERRIES IN ALMOND-LIQUEUR SYRUP

160g brown sugar
80g slivered almonds,
   roasted and finely chopped
80g cold butter, finely chopped
8 just-ripe peaches,
   preferably free-stone
60ml almond-flavoured liqueur
220g raspberries
Mascarpone, to serve

Combine brown sugar and almonds in a bowl, add butter and, using fingertips, rub in butter until mixture resembles coarse breadcrumbs, then cover and refrigerate for 10 minutes.

To remove skins from peaches, blanch peaches, in batches, in a large saucepan of boiling water for 30-60 seconds, depending on ripeness, then plunge immediately into a bowl of ice-cold water. Remove peaches when cool and peel. Halve peaches and remove stones, keeping matching halves together.

Fill each peach cavity with about 1 tablespoon of butter mixture and press halves together to join. Place sandwiched peach halves in a ceramic baking dish just large enough to hold them, sprinkle with remaining butter mixture and drizzle with almond liqueur. Bake at 180C for 20-25 minutes or until peaches are tender. Add raspberries to cooking juice and toss gently to coat.

Spoon peach halves, raspberries and cooking juices into 8 bowls and serve immediately, with marscarpone passed separately.

wine: Bloodwood Ice Riesling, Orange, NSW. Bloodwood risks the elements each year to produce an intensely flavoured but fresh and crisp dessert riesling, made without excessive influence of botrytis that can overpower the true varietal flavours of the riesling grape.

light birthday lunch

CORN SOUP SHOTS

3 corn cobs with husks (about 825g)
1 tablespoon olive oil
1/2 fresh, small red chilli, seeded
 and finely chopped
1 small onion, finely chopped
1 carrot, finely chopped
3 1/2 cups chicken or vegetable stock
 (see basic recipes)
1 cup milk
Red capsicum strips, optional, to serve

Place corn cobs in their husks on a hot barbecue or char-grill and cook for 15 minutes, turning until husks are charred and corn is tender.

When corn is cool enough to handle, remove husks and silks, then cut kernels from cob, reserving both kernels and cobs. Cut each cob into 6.

Heat oil in a large saucepan, add chilli, onion and carrot, stir for 5 minutes, add cobs and stir for another 5 minutes, then add stock and bring to the boil. Simmer over medium heat for 30 minutes. Add milk and stir until heated through, then strain mixture through a fine sieve, pressing down on solids to extract liquid.

Blend strained corn stock and reserved corn kernels in a blender until smooth, push through a fine sieve, then season to taste. Pour mixture into a jug and serve warm in 75ml-capacity shot glasses with capsicum strips, if using.

Makes about 700ml soup.

wine: McWilliam's Oak Aged Amontillado Sherry, Riverina, NSW. Sherry and soup are perfect partners, and the richness of this corn soup demands a full-flavoured yet dry style – amontillado is just that. Lightly chill on a warm day.

time planner

one day ahead: keep covered in refrigerator

- make corn soup
- smoke and sear tuna
- prepare fennel tsatsiki and tabouli
- prepare ricotta topping
- bake meringue cake: keep in airtight container

on the day

- roast tomatoes, make dressing, bring tuna
to room temperature
- heat soup and serve
- prepare lamb and cook
- prepare salad and serve with tuna, tomatoes and dressing
- serve lamb, tsatsiki and tabouli
- assemble meringue cake and serve immediately

What you notice about this meal are its dashing style and great flavours – not the fact that each of its four delicious courses is actually healthily low-fat.

ROSEMARY-SMOKED TUNA, ROASTED-TOMATO, PEPITA AND FETA SALAD

ROSEMARY-SMOKED TUNA, ROASTED-TOMATO, PEPITA AND FETA SALAD

200g (1 cup) white rice
2 bunches of rosemary
3 tuna steaks (about 200g each)
Olive oil
24 small vine-ripened tomatoes
    with calexes (about 60g each)
2 tablespoons balsamic vinegar
200g mixed baby salad leaves
40g (1/4 cup) pepitas, lightly roasted
100g Greek feta, crumbled
Grilled pita bread, to serve

Line a wok with foil, add rice and cover with all but one of the rosemary sprigs, then sprinkle with a little water and heat over medium heat until smoking. Place lightly oiled tuna steaks on a wire rack in base of wok, cover and smoke for 2-3 minutes (tuna will still look raw).

Heat a heavy-based frying pan until very hot, brush tuna lightly with olive oil and season to taste, then cook over high heat for 1-2 minutes (depending on thickness of steaks) on each side until well browned but still rare in the middle, cool to room temperature, then refrigerate until needed.

Remove leaves from remaining rosemary sprig. Place tomatoes in a roasting pan, sprinkle with rosemary, season to taste and drizzle with a little olive oil. Roast at 180C for 20-30 minutes or until soft and skins are just beginning to burst.

Combine balsamic vinegar and 1/3 cup olive oil, season to taste and whisk well.

Combine salad leaves and pepitas in a large bowl, add enough dressing to just coat and toss gently to combine. Slice tuna thinly, add three-quarters to the salad and toss gently. Divide salad mixture among 8 plates, sprinkle with feta, top with remaining sliced tuna and warm roasted tomatoes. Pass grilled pita bread separately.

wine: Ninth Island Pinot Grigio, Tamar Valley, Tas. Pinot Grigio (or pinot gris, as the French call it) is full-flavoured, with savoury and spicy characters powerful enough to balance the smokiness of the tuna with sufficient acid to harmonise with the salad. This is the first release under the Ninth Island label.

LAMB CUTLETS WITH FENNEL TSATSIKI AND TABOULI

Olive oil
3 racks of lamb with 8 cutlets each
    (450g each), trimmed of all fat
2 red capsicum, roasted and peeled
    (see basic recipes)
2 tablespoons pomegranate molasses
1 large clove of garlic, crushed
1½ tablespoons za'atar

FENNEL TSATSIKI

2 bulbs of baby fennel (about 380g),
    trimmed, cored, halved lengthwise
    and very thinly sliced
1 lebanese cucumber, halved,
    seeded and very thinly sliced
2 teaspoons salt
200g Greek-style plain yoghurt
1 tablespoon chopped dill

TABOULI

140g burghul
⅓ cup lemon juice
2 tablespoons extra virgin olive oil
2 cups coarsely chopped
    flat-leaf parsley
50g (⅓ cup) pinenuts, lightly roasted
6 green onions, finely chopped

For fennel tsatsiki, combine fennel, cucumber and salt in a colander and mix well. Stand colander over a bowl for 1 hour, then rinse contents well under water and pat dry with absorbent paper. Combine softened fennel and cucumber with remaining ingredients, mix well and season to taste.

For tabouli, soak burghul in hot water for 20 minutes, then drain well and squeeze out excess water. Combine burghul and remaining ingredients, season to taste and mix well.

Heat 1 tablespoon olive oil in a heavy-based frying pan, add lamb racks, a rack at a time, and sear over high heat until browned. Place lamb and capsicum in a roasting pan, brush lamb with combined pomegranate molasses and garlic, then sprinkle with za'atar. Roast at 200C for 12-15 minutes for medium-rare or until cooked to your liking. Rest lamb and capsicum, loosely covered in a warm place, for 10 minutes. Cut lamb into cutlets and place lamb and capsicum on a bed of tabouli with a spoonful of tsatsiki to one side.

LAMB CUTLETS WITH FENNEL
TSATSIKI AND TABOULI

wine: Penfolds Old Vines Shiraz Mourvèdre, Barossa Valley, SA. The sweet red fruit of shiraz and the savoury, earthy flavours of mourvèdre unencumbered by excessive oak combine to give this Mediterranean-style red great drinkability.

MANGO AND STRAWBERRY MERINGUE CAKE

This meringue cake is crisp on the outside with a marshmallow centre.
4 fresh egg whites at room temperature
180g caster sugar
2 teaspoons cornflour
1 teaspoon white vinegar
500g strawberries, hulled and sliced
2 mangoes (about 1kg), thinly sliced

RICOTTA TOPPING

500g ricotta, drained
80g (½ cup) icing sugar
1 teaspoon grated orange rind
40ml Cointreau or Grand Marnier

For ricotta topping, process ricotta, icing sugar, orange rind and liqueur in a food processor until smooth.

Using an electric mixer, whisk egg whites and a pinch of salt until firm peaks form, then gradually add sugar, whisking between each addition until firm and glossy. Add cornflour and vinegar and whisk until just combined. Spoon mixture into a greased and base-lined 24cm springform pan. Bake at 180C for 5 minutes, then reduce oven temperature to 130C and bake for another 55 minutes or until cake is firm to the touch. Cool in oven with door ajar.

Transfer cooled meringue cake to a cake stand or plate, spread with ricotta mixture, top with strawberries and slices of mango and serve immediately.

wine: Mount Horrocks Cordon Cut Riesling, Clare Valley, SA. Definitive riesling fruit flavours gracefully concentrated on the vine and free of the (usual) overcoat of botrytis make this a good match with the freshness of the fruits in this dessert.

simple outdoor lunch

menu serves 4

shaved veal with tuna and chive mayonnaise

cumin-roasted spatchcock with coriander and red-onion salad

apricot bread and butter pudding

SHAVED VEAL WITH TUNA AND CHIVE MAYONNAISE

Olive oil
1 x 300g fillet of veal
Deep-fried capers, to serve

TUNA AND CHIVE MAYONNAISE
1 cup mayonnaise (see basic recipes)
1 x 95g can tuna in olive oil, drained
1-2 tablespoons lemon juice, to taste
2 tablespoons finely chopped chives

Heat a little olive oil in a flameproof dish and cook veal over high heat until well browned. Roast at 200C for 15 minutes, then cool.

For tuna and chive mayonnaise, process mayonnaise, tuna and lemon juice to taste in a food processor until smooth. Season to taste and stir in chives.

Slice veal paper thin, then place, overlapping, in the centre of 4 plates. Drizzle with tuna and chive mayonnaise and sprinkle with fried capers.

wine: Rosemount Rose Label Chardonnay, Orange, NSW.

CUMIN-ROASTED SPATCHCOCK WITH CORIANDER AND RED-ONION SALAD

2 spatchcocks, quartered
2 tablespoons olive oil
1½ tablespoons ground cumin
2 teaspoons sea salt
¼ cup verjuice
Couscous cooked according to directions on packet and tossed with strips of roasted and peeled red capsicum (see basic recipes) and roasted pinenuts, to serve

CORIANDER AND RED-ONION SALAD
2 cups coriander sprigs
2 tablespoons finely chopped spanish onion
2 teaspoons finely chopped preserved-lemon rind
2 tablespoons olive oil

Rub spatchcock pieces with oil and toss with combined cumin and sea salt. Heat a non-stick frying pan and brown spatchcock over high heat. Transfer to a roasting pan. Deglaze frying pan with verjuice and stir to pick up any sediment. Pour verjuice mixture around spatchcock and roast at 200C for 15 minutes or until tender. Remove spatchcock from pan and rest in a warm place for 5 minutes. Reheat pan juices and season to taste.

For coriander and red-onion salad, combine all ingredients, season to taste and toss gently. Place 2 portions of spatchcock on each plate and top with coriander and red-onion salad. Pass couscous separately.

wine: Seppelt Sunday Creek Pinot Noir, Vic.

APRICOT BREAD AND BUTTER PUDDING

1kg apricots, halved and stoned
1 tablespoon lemon juice
75g (⅓ cup) caster sugar
12 x 1cm-thick brioche slices
75g soft butter, chopped
Roasted flaked almonds and mascarpone or thick cream, to serve

Combine apricots, lemon juice and 55g (¼ cup) sugar in a saucepan and cook, covered, over medium heat until apricots are soft.

Spread brioche with butter, place overlapping slices in an ovenproof dish and sprinkle with remaining sugar. Bake at 200C for 10 minutes or until brioche is golden. Top with apricot mixture and return to oven for 5 minutes. Sprinkle with almonds and serve with mascarpone or thick cream.

wine: Chambers Rosewood Vineyards Light Muscat, Rutherglen, Vic.

You can make most of this lunch hours ahead
– prepare the veal, mayonnaise and salad
vegetables, brown the spatchcock, cook the
apricots and line the pudding dish with brioche.

cocktail party

MINI PAPPADAMS
WITH CUCUMBER
RAITA AND TOMATO
AND CAPSICUM RELISH

time planner

in advance: keep covered in refrigerator

• tomato and capsicum relish can be made up to 1 month ahead

• lime butter can be made 2 weeks ahead

• coconut macaroons can be made 1 week ahead: keep in airtight container

• sesame dipping sauce can be made 3 days ahead

one day ahead: keep covered in refrigerator

• prepare pickled green papaya

• marinate chilli-ginger prawns

• marinate and cook lamb

• marinate chicken

on the day

• prepare cucumber raita

• prepare and steam dumplings, make dipping sauce

• prepare pikelets and barbecued duck

• assemble smoked-salmon rolls

• thread chicken on skewers and grill

• reheat dumplings

• stir-fry prawns

• deep-fry pappadams

• assemble all dishes and serve

MINI PAPPADAMS WITH CUCUMBER RAITA AND TOMATO AND CAPSICUM RELISH

Vegetable oil, for deep-frying
1 x 100g packet mini pappadams

TOMATO AND CAPSICUM RELISH
1 tablespoon vegetable oil
1 small spanish onion, finely chopped
2 teaspoons ground coriander
2 teaspoons cumin seeds
2 cardamom pods, lightly crushed
1 cinnamon stick
2 red capsicum, chopped
2 large ripe tomatoes, chopped
100ml red-wine vinegar
65g (1/3 cup, firmly packed) brown sugar
2 fresh, small red chillies,
    seeded and finely chopped
40g (1/4 cup) sultanas

CUCUMBER RAITA
1 1/2 cups plain yoghurt
1 1/2 lebanese cucumbers
2 teaspoons caster sugar
1 teaspoon white-wine vinegar
1/4 cup finely chopped mint

For tomato and capsicum relish, heat oil in a saucepan, add onion and spices and cook over low heat for 5 minutes. Add capsicum and cook for another 10-15 minutes or until capsicum is soft. Add remaining ingredients and cook over low heat for 30 minutes or until thickened. Spoon into hot sterilised jars, seal while hot and refrigerate for up to 1 month.

For cucumber raita, place yoghurt in a muslin-lined sieve over a bowl and drain for 30 minutes. Grate cucumber, squeeze out excess moisture, then drain on absorbent paper. Combine yoghurt, cucumber and remaining ingredients, season to taste and mix well. Cover and refrigerate for up to 8 hours.

Heat vegetable oil in a deep frying pan and fry pappadams, in batches, until puffed and golden. Drain on absorbent paper. Cool and store in a sealed plastic bag until ready to use.

Spoon tomato and capsicum relish and cucumber raita into separate bowls and serve with pappadams.

Makes about 2 3/4 cups tomato and capsicum relish and about 1 1/2 cups cucumber raita.

This menu provides generous amounts of cocktail food for 30, but it may suit you better to make just three or four of the recipes. In that case, increase the quantities – the caterer's rule of thumb is to allow seven to 10 'bites' per person.

CARROT, ZUCCHINI AND GINGER PIKELETS
WITH BARBECUED DUCK; SMOKED-SALMON
ROLLS WITH PICKLED GREEN PAWPAW

PORK AND PRAWN DUMPLINGS WITH
DIPPING SAUCE; CHILLI-GINGER PRAWNS

CARROT, ZUCCHINI AND GINGER PIKELETS WITH BARBECUED DUCK

150g (1 cup) self-raising flour
65g (1/3 cup) rice flour
1 egg, lightly beaten
1 cup milk
1 small carrot, grated
1 small zucchini, grated
1 tablespoon finely grated ginger
25g butter, melted
4 green onions, thinly sliced
    on the diagonal

BARBECUED DUCK
1/2 barbecued chinese duck
1 1/2 tablespoons hoisin sauce
3 teaspoons white vinegar
1/4 teaspoon chinese five-spice powder
20g (1/4 cup) beansprouts

For barbecued duck, remove skin and flesh from duck and slice thinly. Discard fat and bones. Combine hoisin sauce, vinegar and spice and mix well. Combine duck, sauce mixture and beansprouts, season to taste and mix well.

Combine flours in a bowl, make a well in the centre and carefully whisk in combined egg and milk and mix until smooth. Add carrot, zucchini and ginger and mix well. Stir in butter and season to taste with salt.

Heat a heavy-based non-stick frying pan, add tablespoonfuls of pikelet mixture and cook, in batches, over medium heat until bubbles appear on surface and burst. Turn over and cook for another minute or until golden. Repeat with remaining mixture.

Top pikelets with duck mixture and sprinkle with green onion.

Makes about 45 pikelets.

SMOKED-SALMON ROLLS WITH PICKLED GREEN PAWPAW

1/2 green pawpaw
    (about 500g), julienned
1/2 daikon (about 250g),
    peeled and julienned
1/2 cup seasoned rice-wine vinegar
1/2 cup mirin
2 tablespoons lime juice
8 green onions, julienned
500g large slices of smoked salmon
1/2 cup thai basil leaves
1/2 cup coriander leaves

Combine pawpaw and daikon in a bowl, pour combined vinegar, mirin and lime juice over and stand for 2-3 hours. Add green onion, toss to combine, then drain.

Cut smoked-salmon slices in half crosswise, then top each half with 2 leaves each of thai basil and coriander. Top with a few pickled vegetables and roll up tightly. Smoked-salmon rolls can be assembled up to 6 hours in advance. Cover and refrigerate until ready to use.

Makes about 40.

PORK AND PRAWN DUMPLINGS WITH DIPPING SAUCE

350g minced pork
200g uncooked prawns, peeled,
    deveined and finely chopped
1 teaspoon grated ginger
1 clove of garlic, finely chopped
6 green onions, finely chopped
1 1/2 teaspoons soy sauce
2 x 275g packets gow gee wrappers

DIPPING SAUCE
1/2 cup soy sauce
1/3 cup shaohsing rice wine
1 tablespoon ginger juice
1 tablespoon honey

For dipping sauce, combine all ingredients in a small saucepan and stir over low heat until honey dissolves. Cool.

Combine pork, prawn, ginger, garlic, green onion and soy sauce in a bowl and mix well. Place 12 gow gee wrappers on a clean surface. Spoon 2 teaspoons of mixture on one half of each wrapper. Brush edge with water and fold pastry over to form a half-moon, then pinch edges together to seal. Repeat with remaining wrappers and filling. Place dumplings on a baking-paper-lined oven tray, cover with plastic wrap and refrigerate for up to 8 hours.

Place dumplings in a baking-paper-lined bamboo steamer, making sure dumplings do not touch each other. Brush edge of each dumpling with water, cover steamer, then place over a wok of boiling water and steam for 5-6 minutes. Serve with dipping sauce. Dumplings can be cooked in advance and reheated by steaming.

Makes about 45.

CHILLI-GINGER PRAWNS

8 cloves of garlic, finely chopped
1/3 cup finely grated ginger
3 fresh, small red chillies, finely chopped
1 cup coriander, coarsely chopped
2 tablespoons chopped lemongrass
2 teaspoons chinese five-spice powder
2 tablespoons lime juice
2 teaspoons chopped fresh turmeric
    or 1/2 teaspoon turmeric powder
1/2 cup olive oil
1.5kg medium uncooked prawns
    (about 60), peeled and deveined,
    leaving tails intact
Peanut oil, for stir-frying
2 tablespoons lime juice, extra

Process garlic, ginger, chilli, coriander, lemongrass, spice, lime juice and turmeric in a food processor until finely chopped. Add oil and process until a paste forms. Place prawns in a glass or ceramic dish, add paste and mix well to coat prawns. Cover and refrigerate for 4-6 hours or overnight. Stand prawns at room temperature for 30 minutes before cooking.

Heat a wok over high heat, add 2 tablespoons peanut oil and stir-fry prawns, in batches, over high heat for 3-4 minutes until prawns change colour, wiping wok clean when necessary and adding more oil as needed. Drizzle with extra lime juice and serve immediately.

SPICY LAMB WITH MANGO CHUTNEY ON TURKISH BREAD

1/2 cup korma curry paste
1/3 cup plain yoghurt
1 tablespoon lemon juice
1kg lamb backstraps
2 turkish bread loaves, split lengthwise
Olive oil
1/2 cup mango chutney
Plain yoghurt, extra, to serve
1/4 cup small mint leaves

Combine curry paste, yoghurt and lemon juice in a glass or ceramic bowl and mix well. Add lamb and turn to coat well. Cover and refrigerate for 3-4 hours.

Place lamb on a rack in a roasting pan and roast at 200C for 25 minutes for medium. Stand for 10 minutes before cutting into 1cm-thick slices or cover and refrigerate (return meat to room temperature before slicing).

Brush top and base of turkish bread with oil and grill for 1-2 minutes or until just crisp and golden. Cut turkish bread into 10cm squares, then cut each square into 4 triangles. Spread a little mango chutney on each triangle, top with a slice of lamb and a small dollop of extra yoghurt and finish with a mint leaf.

TERIYAKI CHICKEN SKEWERS WITH SESAME DIPPING SAUCE

4 chicken breast fillets
1/4 cup japanese soy sauce
1 1/2 tablespoons mirin
2 teaspoons cooking sake
2 teaspoons caster sugar
60 small bamboo skewers,
    soaked in cold water for 30 minutes

SESAME DIPPING SAUCE
90g (1/2 cup) sesame seeds
2 tablespoons mirin
1/4 cup soy sauce
3 teaspoons sugar
1/3 cup vegetable stock
    (see basic recipes)

For sesame dipping sauce, heat a non-stick frying pan, add sesame seeds and cook, shaking pan regularly, over low-medium heat until seeds are golden. Transfer seeds to a mortar, add mirin and grind to a paste with a pestle. Transfer to a bowl and stir in remaining ingredients. Store in a screw-top jar and refrigerate for up to 3 days.

Thinly slice chicken lengthwise and place in a glass or ceramic bowl. Combine soy sauce, mirin, sake and sugar, pour marinade over chicken and turn chicken to coat. Cover and refrigerate for 3-4 hours or overnight. Drain chicken and reserve marinade. Thread 1-2 chicken pieces (depending on size) onto each skewer. Skewers can be covered and refrigerated for up to 4 hours at this stage. Grill chicken under medium heat for 2-3 minutes on each side, brushing occasionally with reserved marinade. Serve immediately with sesame dipping sauce.

Makes about 60.

COCONUT MACAROONS WITH LIME BUTTER

90g (1 cup) desiccated coconut
2 egg whites
110g (1/2 cup) caster sugar
65g (1/4 cup) light palm sugar
35g (1/4 cup) plain flour
2 teaspoons grated lime rind
1 pawpaw, thinly sliced
Zested rind of 1 lime

LIME BUTTER
2 egg yolks
55g (1/4 cup) caster sugar
1 teaspoon grated lime rind
1/4 cup lime juice
70g unsalted butter, chopped

For lime butter, whisk egg yolks, sugar and lime rind in the top of a double boiler or in a heatproof bowl over simmering water until sugar dissolves and mixture is pale. Stir in lime juice and mix well. Gradually add butter, piece by piece, stirring until each piece has melted. Continue to stir until mixture thickens and coats the back of a wooden spoon. Do not boil. Cool.

Place coconut on an oven tray and roast at 160C, shaking tray regularly, for 10 minutes or until golden.

Using an electric mixer, beat egg whites until frothy, add caster sugar 2 tablespoons at a time, beating between each addition until sugar dissolves. Add palm sugar 1 tablespoon at a time and beat until mixture is thick and glossy and firm peaks form. Add cooled roasted coconut, flour and lime rind and beat until well combined. Place 1/2 tablespoons of mixture at 5cm intervals on 2 baking-paper-lined oven trays and spread to form 3cm discs. Bake at 140C for 40 minutes or until dry, swapping trays from top to bottom after 20 minutes. Cool in oven with door ajar.

Top each macaroon with a little lime butter, a slice of pawpaw and some zested lime rind.

Makes about 45.

wines: Here are some suggestions for what to drink with these dishes. **Seaview Pinot Noir Chardonnay Brut, SA.** This rich and generously flavoured sparkling wine combines the powerful red berry fruit flavours and firm structure of pinot noir with the elegance and zest of chardonnay. It's rich enough to act as "food" sparkling wine. **Orlando St Helga Riesling, Eden Valley, SA.** Riesling remains the most versatile grape variety, combining harmoniously with the freshness of cucumber, the acid of tomato, the spiciness of ginger and the sweetness of seafood – in short, the perfect party white. This St Helga is an often overlooked gem. **Montrose Barbera, Mudgee, NSW.** Barbera is a lesser known variety within Australia, but it is big in its homeland, Italy, and more recently in California. Its savoury fruit flavours of dark cherry and prunes and its refreshing acidity make it a useful wine with lighter meat dishes and Asian spices. The Montrose plantings were among the first in Australia.

COCONUT MACAROONS WITH LIME BUTTER

smart dinner party

SMOKED-TROUT LINGUINE

1 large smoked trout (about 300g)
50g (1 cup) baby spinach
   leaves, trimmed
6 green onions, thinly sliced
   on the diagonal
1/2 cup chervil leaves
400g fresh linguine
Olive oil
Extra chervil leaves, to serve

DRESSING

1/2 cup extra virgin olive oil
1 1/2 tablespoons lemon juice
1/4 cup orange juice
1 teaspoon dijon mustard
1 teaspoon sugar

For dressing, combine all ingredients in a small bowl and whisk well, then season with sea salt and cracked black pepper.

Remove skin and bones from trout, flake flesh into large pieces and combine with spinach, green onion and chervil. Add half the dressing and toss to combine.

Cook linguine in boiling, salted water with a splash of olive oil for 2-3 minutes or until al dente, then drain and toss with remaining dressing.

Place linguine on 6 plates, top with trout mixture and scatter with extra chervil leaves.

wine: Cullen Classic Dry White, Margaret River, WA. Most "classic dry whites" are lightly flavoured and have fresh herbal characters, relying on semillon and sauvignon blanc as their varietal base. Unfortunately, too many are somewhat sweet rather than dry, but not so this excellent Cullen wine, a definitive example of the style.

time planner

one day ahead: keep covered in refrigerator

• prepare pastry, line tin and freeze, prepare ricotta filling

• make dressing for pasta

on the day

• assemble and bake tart and cool

• prepare and bake sweet-potato boulangère

• prepare veal parcels and salad

• flake trout, cook linguine and serve

• cook veal parcels and serve with salad and boulangère

• serve tart

There are two 'treasure' recipes in this menu – the tart pastry, which is outstanding for savoury as well as sweet uses, and the smoked-trout linguine for brilliantly easy yet elegant lunches and suppers.

RICOTTA AND BERRY TART

VEAL, BOCCONCINI AND PROSCIUTTO PARCELS

6 veal topside steaks (about 150g each)
6 bocconcini, sliced
1/4 cup oregano leaves
Lemon-pressed extra virgin olive oil
    or extra virgin olive oil
12 slices prosciutto
1/2 cup verjuice
1/2 cup chicken stock (see basic recipes)
1/3 cup pouring cream
Pea and rocket salad, to serve

Place veal steaks between 2 sheets of plastic wrap and flatten with the smooth side of a meat mallet until 5mm thick. Place bocconcini slices on one half of each veal steak, scatter with oregano, season to taste and drizzle with lemon-pressed extra virgin olive oil. Fold other side of veal over and tuck end under, then wrap 2 slices of prosciutto crosswise around each parcel to cover opening.

Heat a lightly oiled non-stick frying pan and cook parcels for 1-2 minutes on each side until browned, then transfer to an oven tray and bake at 180C for 6-8 minutes. Reserve frying pan. Remove parcels from oven and rest in a warm place for 5 minutes.

Deglaze reserved pan with verjuice and stock and simmer until reduced by half. Add cream and simmer until reduced and slightly thickened, then season to taste.

Cut veal parcels in half and serve with sweet-potato boulangère (recipe follows) and pea and rocket salad. Pass sauce separately.

SWEET-POTATO BOULANGERE

1.5kg purple, orange and white
    sweet potato, peeled and cut
    into 3mm-thick slices
8 cloves of garlic, thinly sliced
2 tablespoons thyme leaves
80g butter, chopped
1 cup chicken stock (see basic recipes)
1 tablespoon olive oil

Butter an 8-cup-capacity ovenproof dish. Place purple sweet potato over base of dish, scatter with half the garlic and thyme and dot with 30g butter, then drizzle with 1/3 cup chicken stock and season to taste. Repeat with orange sweet potato, remaining garlic and thyme, 30g butter and 1/3 cup chicken stock, then top with white sweet potato, dot with remaining butter, pour remaining chicken stock over and season to taste. Cover with foil and bake at 180C for 20 minutes, then remove foil, brush top with olive oil and bake for another 40-50 minutes or until potato is tender and golden around edges.

wine: Lindemans Padthaway Pinot Noir, Padthaway, SA. Veal has subtle flavours, as does bocconcini, so a bold red would overpower this dish. Pinot is perfect – the sweet red berry fruit flavours counterpoint the saltiness of the prosciutto and the sweetness of the vegetable accompaniment.

VEAL, BOCCONCINI AND
PROSCIUTTO PARCELS

RICOTTA AND BERRY TART

240g plain flour
180g cold unsalted butter, chopped
1 teaspoon cinnamon sugar
120g raspberries
120g blueberries
Thick cream, to serve

RICOTTA FILLING

1/2 vanilla bean, split lengthwise
250g ricotta
110g (1/2 cup) caster sugar
Grated rind of 1 lemon and 1 orange
40ml overproof dark rum
1/2 cup thickened cream
1 1/2 tablespoons lemon juice
2 x 67g eggs
1 teaspoon cornflour

For ricotta filling, scrape seeds from vanilla bean and reserve bean for another use. Process remaining ingredients with vanilla seeds in a food processor until smooth.

Sift flour and a pinch of salt onto a surface, toss butter in flour to coat lightly, then, using fingertips, rub in lightly until it just begins to be incorporated. Make a well in the centre of mixture, add 70ml cold water and, using a flat plastic or metal pastry cutter, gradually mix flour into water until mixture is a mass of buttery balls of dough. Using the heel of your hand, spread pastry across bench until mixture just comes together. Form into a disc, wrap in plastic wrap and refrigerate for 3 hours.

Roll out dough on a lightly floured surface until 3mm thick, then line a 23cm tart tin with removable base. Carefully press pastry into side of tin and trim pastry so it extends 5mm above edge of tart tin. Cover and refrigerate overnight or freeze for at least 4 hours. Line pastry with baking paper, fill with dried beans or rice and bake blind at 180C for 35 minutes, then remove paper and bake pastry for another 5 minutes. Sprinkle hot pastry case with half the cinnamon sugar and pour in filling, top with raspberries and blueberries and sprinkle with remaining cinnamon sugar. Bake at 180C for 35-40 minutes until filling is just firm around edge but still slightly wobbly in the centre. Cool tart to room temperature and serve with thick cream.

wine: Tollana Botrytis Riesling, Eden Valley, SA. Eden Valley's cool climate is perfect for late-ripening grape varieties, such as riesling, especially when the winemaker wants to make a botrytis-affected dessert wine. Tollana is much undervalued – this wine is a beauty.

sunday barbecue lunch

menu serves 12

chicken-liver pâté with toasts and cornichons

barbecued haloumi and asparagus with lemon salsa verde

char-grilled octopus with hummus and roasted-vegetable salad

barbecued whole rump with panzanella

rocket and pumpkin salad

macadamia, coconut and star-anise praline with tropical fruits

CHICKEN-LIVER PATE WITH TOASTS AND CORNICHONS

time planner

one day ahead: keep covered in refrigerator

- make chicken-liver pâté
- bake toasts: keep in airtight container
- make hummus, roast vegetables, prepare dressing
- blend anchovy butter
- roast and peel capsicum for panzanella
- prepare macadamia praline: keep in airtight container

on the day

- marinate whole rump, marinate octopus
- roast pumpkin for salad, prepare leaves and dressing
- prepare lemon salsa verde
- roast or barbecue rump
- prepare tropical fruit salad
- serve pâté and toasts
- barbecue or pan-fry asparagus and haloumi and serve
- barbecue or char-grill octopus and serve
- prepare panzanella and rocket and pumpkin salad
- serve main course and salads, then dessert

CHICKEN-LIVER PATE WITH TOASTS AND CORNICHONS

80g butter, chopped
1 large onion (about 300g), chopped
500g chicken liver, cleaned and trimmed
20ml brandy
2 eggs, boiled for 5 minutes,
    then cooled, peeled and chopped
1 teaspoon sea salt
1/2 baguette
Cornichons, to serve

Melt half the butter in a large frying pan, add onion and cook, over very low heat, for 15 minutes or until soft and golden. Add remaining butter and chicken liver and stir over medium heat for 4 minutes, then stir in brandy and cook for another minute or until chicken liver is just cooked. Cool.

Combine chicken-liver mixture, egg and sea salt in a food processor and process, using the pulse button, until a coarse paste forms. Season to taste with cracked black pepper. Cover and refrigerate until ready to use.

Thinly slice baguette on the diagonal and place bread on oven trays. Bake at 180C for 10 minutes or until golden and crisp, turning after 5 minutes.

Serve chicken-liver pâté with toasts and cornichons.

For a barbecue, it's always a good idea to have something ready to offer as soon as guests arrive. Rich chicken-liver toasts will keep everyone happy until the haloumi and asparagus and the octopus appear, with the beef as a magnificent climax.

BARBECUED HALOUMI
AND ASPARAGUS
WITH LEMON SALSA VERDE

CHAR-GRILLED OCTOPUS
WITH ROASTED-VEGETABLE
SALAD AND HUMMUS

BARBECUED HALOUMI AND ASPARAGUS WITH LEMON SALSA VERDE

24 asparagus spears, trimmed
6 bamboo skewers, soaked
   in hot water for 15 minutes
800g haloumi, thickly sliced
Olive oil
3 lemons, thickly sliced

LEMON SALSA VERDE

1 1/2 cups flat-leaf parsley, finely chopped
3/4 cup mint leaves, finely chopped
3/4 cup basil leaves, finely chopped
1/4 cup capers, rinsed and drained
3 cloves of garlic, crushed
1 cup olive oil
90ml lemon juice

For lemon salsa verde, combine herbs, capers and garlic in a bowl and gradually whisk in oil, then lemon juice, and season to taste.

Thread 4 asparagus spears onto each skewer. Brush asparagus and haloumi generously with oil.

Barbecue asparagus for 2 minutes on each side or until just tender. Barbecue haloumi on a hot plate for 2 minutes on each side or until golden, then barbecue lemon slices until caramelised. Remove skewers, place asparagus on a large plate, top with haloumi and lemon slices, drizzle with half the lemon salsa verde and pass remaining salsa separately. Serve immediately.

CHAR-GRILLED OCTOPUS WITH ROASTED-VEGETABLE SALAD AND HUMMUS

2kg cleaned baby octopus,
   halved if large
1 1/2 red capsicum, cut into 2cm pieces
2 small eggplant, cut into 2cm pieces
3 spanish onions, each cut
   into 8 wedges
3 zucchini, cut into 2cm-thick slices
Olive oil
1 cup flat-leaf parsley and basil leaves
1 1/2 cups hummus (see basic recipes)

AGED-BALSAMIC DRESSING

2/3 cup olive oil
2 tablespoons aged balsamic vinegar
2 cloves of garlic, chopped

For aged-balsamic dressing, combine all ingredients and season to taste.

Place baby octopus in a glass or ceramic dish, pour half the dressing over and marinate, covered, in the refrigerator for at least 1 hour.

Combine capsicum, eggplant, onion and zucchini in a roasting pan, drizzle with oil and roast at 200C, turning once, for 30 minutes or until vegetables are browned and tender. Cool slightly and toss gently with mixed herbs.

Char-grill or barbecue drained octopus over high heat until just cooked. Spread hummus on a large plate, top with roasted-vegetable salad and octopus and drizzle with remaining dressing.

BARBECUED WHOLE RUMP WITH PANZANELLA

1 x 3kg whole rump of beef
2 cloves of garlic, chopped
1 tablespoon thyme leaves
2 tablespoons olive oil
2 tablespoons aged balsamic vinegar

ANCHOVY BUTTER

8 anchovy fillets, drained and chopped
2 cloves of garlic, chopped
2 tablespoons chopped flat-leaf parsley
1 tablespoon chopped thyme leaves
250g soft butter, chopped

PANZANELLA

1/4 cup red-wine vinegar
2/3 cup extra virgin olive oil
1 Italian-style bread loaf, crusts removed
    and bread cut into 2cm pieces
10 vine-ripened tomatoes, peeled,
    seeded and cut into wedges
3 red and 3 yellow capsicum,
    roasted and peeled
    (see basic recipes)
2 tablespoons rinsed salted capers
2 shallots, sliced
1 cup torn basil leaves
1 x 125g jar small black olives, drained

Rub rump all over with combined garlic, thyme, oil and vinegar and stand at room temperature for 1 hour. Sprinkle with cracked black pepper and sea salt and barbecue in a covered barbecue over medium heat for about 1 1/2 hours for medium-rare, or place in a roasting pan and roast in the oven at 200C for 1 1/2 hours. Rest in a warm place for 15 minutes before slicing.

For anchovy butter, process all ingredients in a food processor until smooth. Transfer to a dish, cover and refrigerate until ready to serve.

For panzanella, combine vinegar and oil and season to taste. Ten minutes before serving, place dressing and remaining ingredients in a large bowl and toss gently to combine.

Serve slices of rump topped with anchovy butter and accompanied by panzanella and rocket and pumpkin salad (recipe follows).

ROCKET AND PUMPKIN SALAD

3kg queensland blue pumpkin,
    peeled and cut into 2cm pieces
Olive oil
200g rocket
200g goat's feta
2 tablespoons white-wine vinegar

Place pumpkin in a roasting pan, drizzle with olive oil and roast at 200C for 35 minutes, turning once, until well browned and crisp.

Place rocket in a large salad bowl, top with pumpkin, crumble feta over, sprinkle with cracked black pepper and sea salt and drizzle with 1/2 cup olive oil combined with vinegar.

MACADAMIA, COCONUT AND STAR-ANISE PRALINE WITH TROPICAL FRUITS

50g macadamia halves, lightly roasted
30g flaked coconut, lightly roasted
200g caster sugar
3 star anise

TROPICAL FRUITS

2 pawpaws, halved and sliced
3 mangoes, cheeks removed and sliced
3 oranges, halved lengthwise and sliced
1 pineapple, cored and sliced
60ml white rum
90ml lime juice
4 kaffir-lime leaves, thinly sliced

MACADAMIA, COCONUT AND STAR-ANISE PRALINE WITH TROPICAL FRUITS

Spread macadamia and coconut in a single layer on a lightly greased oven tray. Combine sugar, star anise and 1/2 cup water in a small, heavy-based saucepan and stir over low heat until sugar dissolves. Increase heat and boil, without stirring, until mixture is just beginning to change colour. Remove star anise and cook until syrup turns a caramel colour. Remove from heat and pour over macadamia and coconut on oven tray. Cool until hard, then break into 4cm pieces.

For tropical fruits, combine all ingredients and half the praline, then cover and refrigerate for 30 minutes for flavours to develop.

Divide tropical fruits among 12 small bowls or place in one large bowl and top with remaining praline.

wines: Here are some suggestions for what to drink with these dishes. **Julian Chivite Gran Feudo Rosado, Navarra, Spain.** This grenache-based rosé is a classic from Navarra, situated on the high plateau of northern Spain. Candy pink with a full flavour of wild cherries, it has a slash of acid and a hint of tannin which help to cut through the richness of the chicken liver. **Martinez Bujanda Garnacha Reserva, Rioja, Spain.** While tempranillo is the main variety of the Rioja, grenache (or garnacha, as it is known in Spain) is also widely planted. It produces a robust red wine with a firm tannin structure which helps this wine to match the strong "meatiness" and the charry flavours of the barbecued beef. **Bodegas Vinicola Hidalgo Oloroso Napoleon Seco, Jerez, Spain.** The Spanish produce oloroso sherries with a rich and intense flavour and a semi-dry finish, in marked contrast to the much sweeter Australian versions. This Hidalgo has a natural nutty flavour from its time in old oak barrels, and it will make a brilliant pairing with this dessert.

simple light dinner

OYSTERS WITH GINGER AND SHALLOT DRESSING

24 rock oysters, freshly shucked
24 coriander leaves

GINGER AND SHALLOT DRESSING
1 shallot, finely chopped
1 teaspoon grated ginger
1/4 cup ponzu
1 tablespoon lime juice
1/4 teaspoon sesame oil, or to taste

For ginger and shallot dressing, combine all ingredients and season to taste.

Place oysters on a large plate and top each with a coriander leaf. Just before serving, spoon a little dressing over.
wine: Taylors Clare Riesling, Clare Valley, SA.

MARINATED QUAIL WITH CHINESE-CABBAGE SALAD

1/4 cup soy sauce
1 tablespoon shaohsing rice wine
    or sherry
1 teaspoon brown sugar
2 cloves of garlic, chopped
2 fresh, small red chillies,
    seeded and chopped, or to taste
4 quail, quartered
Peanut oil
Steamed rice, cooked
    with cardamom pods, to serve

CHINESE-CABBAGE SALAD
1 spanish onion, finely chopped
1/2 chinese cabbage (about 500g),
    finely shredded
1 tablespoon finely chopped
    vietnamese mint
1 tablespoon finely chopped coriander
2 tablespoons rice vinegar
1 teaspoon brown sugar
1 tablespoon lime juice

Combine soy sauce, rice wine, sugar, garlic and chilli to taste and pour over quail. Marinate, covered, in refrigerator for at least 30 minutes or overnight.

For chinese-cabbage salad, sprinkle onion with a little salt, stand for 30 minutes, then rinse and drain. Combine onion and cabbage, toss with combined remaining ingredients and season to taste.

Heat a little peanut oil in a wok or large frying pan until hot and stir-fry drained quail, in batches, until browned and tender.

Serve quail on a bed of chinese-cabbage salad and pass rice separately.
wine: Scotchmans Hill Pinot Noir, Bellarine Peninsula, Vic.

ORANGE SORBET WITH HONEYDEW MELON

300g (1 1/3 cups) caster sugar
1 teaspoon grated orange rind
3 cups fresh orange juice
    (about 7-8 oranges),
    strained and simmered
    until reduced to 2 cups
1/2 large or 1 small honeydew melon
    (about 1kg), peeled and chopped
    into 5mm pieces

Combine sugar and 1 1/3 cups water in a saucepan and simmer over medium heat until sugar dissolves. Stir in orange rind and cool to room temperature.

Combine sugar syrup and cooled reduced orange juice, mix well and freeze in an ice-cream maker according to manufacturer's instructions.

Serve scoops of orange sorbet topped with chopped melon.
wine: Chandon Cuvée Riche, Yarra Valley, Vic.

This is the right meal for a warm evening – light, refreshing and easy on the cook. Start the sorbet churning just before you sit down to eat and it will be ready when you want it.

christmas celebration

time planner

in advance: keep covered in refrigerator

• lime curd can be made 2 weeks ahead

one day ahead: keep covered in refrigerator

• make smoked-trout mousse

• prepare macadamia-herb stuffing

• bake mini tart shells: keep in airtight container

on the day

• prepare filling, bake cake, make mascarpone cream

• prepare cucumber salad

• roast vegetables

• stuff and prepare turkey breast and roast

• serve cucumber salad with smoked-trout mousse

• reheat vegetables, prepare watercress salad, serve turkey

• serve cake

• assemble tarts and serve

SMOKED-TROUT MOUSSE WITH CUCUMBER SALAD

2 smoked trout, skin and bones
    removed to give 400g flesh
300g sour cream
1/4 cup lemon juice
1/4 cup thickened cream
1 teaspoon bottled horseradish
17g gelatine leaves
1 cup chicken stock (see basic recipes)
1-2 telegraph cucumbers,
    thinly sliced lengthwise

CUCUMBER SALAD

4 lebanese cucumbers,
    thinly sliced on the diagonal
1 teaspoon sea salt
1 teaspoon white-wine vinegar
2 teaspoons olive oil
1 tablespoon finely chopped mint

Process trout flesh in a food processor until finely chopped, add sour cream, lemon juice, cream and horseradish and season to taste. Process until combined and smooth.

Soak gelatine leaves in cold water for 3 minutes until soft, then drain and squeeze out excess liquid.

Heat stock until simmering, then remove from heat, stir in gelatine leaves and stand for 10 minutes. Stir stock mixture into smoked-trout mixture and stand for 15 minutes. Place 8-9 slices of cucumber over base and ends of a lightly oiled 13x21cm loaf tin, carefully spoon smoked-trout mixture over cucumber, cover with plastic wrap and refrigerate for 4 hours or overnight.

For cucumber salad, place cucumber in a colander, sprinkle with sea salt and stand for 30 minutes. Pat cucumber dry with absorbent paper, then toss with vinegar, oil and mint.

Serve slices of smoked-trout mousse with cucumber salad.

wine: Shaw and Smith Sauvignon Blanc, Adelaide Hills, SA. Sauvignon blanc has the freshness and the herbal fruit flavours which combine well with the freshness of the cucumber and the intensity of the smoked trout. Shaw and Smith produces one of Australia's best sauvignons.

All the good things that say Christmas – an elegant seafood starter, turkey with roasted vegetables, a divinely rich fruit-filled cake – plotted for minimum effort on the day and for ease of serving.

SMOKED-TROUT MOUSSE WITH CUCUMBER SALAD

ROASTED TURKEY BREAST WITH MACADAMIA-HERB STUFFING

15g soft butter
1 teaspoon chopped sage
1 x 1.6kg turkey breast with skin on
3/4 cup chicken stock (see basic recipes)
1/2 cup cranberry sauce
1 teaspoon worcestershire sauce

MACADAMIA-HERB STUFFING

40g butter, chopped
1 small onion, finely chopped
2 bacon rashers, chopped
40g macadamias, chopped
50g (3/4 cup) day-old breadcrumbs
1/3 cup grated pear
1 1/2 tablespoons chopped sage
1 1/2 tablespoons sweetened
   dried cranberries

For macadamia-herb stuffing, melt butter in a frying pan, add onion and cook over low heat for 5 minutes, then add bacon and macadamia and cook for another 3 minutes or until lightly browned. Transfer mixture to a bowl, stir in remaining ingredients and season to taste. Cool to room temperature.

Mix butter and sage and season to taste. Carefully lift skin from turkey breast, spread butter mixture over flesh, then press skin back down. Place breast, skin side down, on bench, place stuffing in centre, then fold sides together. Using kitchen string, tie breast at 2cm intervals to form a uniform shape.

Place turkey in a lightly greased roasting pan and roast at 180C, basting regularly, for 50-60 minutes or until juices run clear when thickest part is pierced with a skewer. Remove turkey from pan, cover with foil and rest in a warm place for 15 minutes.

Skim fat from pan juices, place over medium heat, add chicken stock, cranberry sauce and worcestershire sauce and simmer for 5 minutes or until reduced and slightly thickened, then season to taste.

Serve sliced turkey with sauce, accompanied by roasted vegetables and watercress and avocado salad (recipes follow).

ROASTED VEGETABLES

Vegetables can be roasted ahead of time and returned to oven for 15 minutes at 180C to heat through while turkey is resting.

750g desirée potatoes, cut into wedges
Olive oil
600g parsnips, cut into 8cm-long pieces
750g sweet potato, cut into 8cm wedges
3 red capsicum, cut into 2cm-thick slices
3 yellow capsicum,
   cut into 2cm-thick slices
3 leeks, halved lengthwise
   and cut into 8cm lengths
1 tablespoon thyme leaves

Place potato in a large roasting pan, drizzle with a little oil, season with sea salt and roast at 200C for 20 minutes. Add parsnip and sweet potato, drizzle with a little more oil, check seasoning and roast for another 45 minutes or until vegetables are tender, browned and crisp.

Meanwhile, place capsicum and leek in another roasting pan, drizzle with 2 tablespoons olive oil, sprinkle with thyme and season to taste, then roast at 200C on bottom shelf of oven for 45 minutes.

WATERCRESS AND AVOCADO SALAD

2 cups picked watercress leaves
1 red oak-leaf lettuce, leaves removed
   and torn into pieces
200g sugarsnap peas, blanched
   in boiling water for 30 seconds,
   then drained
1 avocado, peeled and sliced

DRESSING

1/3 cup extra virgin olive oil
1 1/2 tablespoons apple-cider vinegar
1/2 teaspoon dijon mustard

For dressing, combine all ingredients, season to taste and whisk well.

Combine leaves, sugarsnaps and avocado in a bowl, pour dressing over and toss gently.

wine: Peter Rumball Sparkling Shiraz, SA. Australia has very few of its own Christmas traditions, but pairing turkey with sparkling shiraz is one of them. And it's entirely valid, not just a blind tradition – just try it.

BUTTER CAKE WITH CANDIED-FRUIT FILLING AND GRAND MARNIER SYRUP

200g soft butter, chopped
100g caster sugar
2 teaspoons finely grated lemon rind
2 eggs
260g (1 3/4) cups self-raising flour
1 teaspoon baking powder
1/2 cup milk
Sliced candied mandarin, optional,
   to serve

CANDIED-FRUIT FILLING

150g (1/3 cup) chopped
   candied mandarin
120g (1/4 cup) chopped
   candied orange rind
55g (1/3 cup) sultanas
50g (1/3 cup) sweetened
   dried cranberries
40ml Grand Marnier

MASCARPONE CREAM

250g mascarpone
1/2 cup thickened cream
1 tablespoon icing sugar
40ml Grand Marnier

GRAND MARNIER SYRUP

55g (1/4 cup) caster sugar
100ml strained orange juice
40ml Grand Marnier

For candied-fruit filling, combine all ingredients, mix well and stand for 2 hours.

For mascarpone cream, combine all ingredients in a bowl and whisk until soft peaks form. Do not over-whisk.

Beat butter, sugar and lemon rind until light and fluffy, add eggs, one at a time,

BUTTER CAKE WITH
CANDIED-FRUIT FILLING AND
GRAND MARNIER SYRUP

beating well after each. Add combined sifted flour and baking powder alternately with milk, in 2 batches, and mix until well combined. Spoon half the mixture into a greased and base-lined round 22cm cake tin, spoon filling over and top with remaining mixture. Bake at 180C for 1 hour or until cooked when tested with a skewer. Stand cake in tin for 5 minutes before turning out onto a wire rack to cool.

Meanwhile, for Grand Marnier syrup, combine sugar, strained orange juice and 1/4 cup water in a small saucepan and stir over low heat until sugar dissolves, then simmer for 3 minutes. Add liqueur and simmer for another 1-2 minutes or until slightly reduced. Pour hot syrup over warm cake and decorate top of cake with sliced candied mandarins, if using. Serve slices of cake warm or at room temperature with mascarpone cream.

wine: Brown Brothers Late Harvested Orange Flora and Muscat, Milawa, Vic. Most dessert wines produced in Australia are too sweet to pair well with desserts that rely on fresh fruit and citrus flavours. This quirky combination of varieties delivers a flavoursome but not overly sweet wine – a perfect match for this dish.

MINIATURE TARTS WITH LIME CURD, MANGO AND RASPBERRIES

225g (1 1/2 cups) plain flour
2 tablespoons icing sugar
2 tablespoons desiccated coconut
85g cold butter, chopped
1 egg, lightly beaten
1 mango, thinly sliced
   with a vegetable peeler
120g raspberries
Icing sugar, for dusting

LIME CURD

4 egg yolks
110g (1/2 cup) caster sugar
1 tablespoon grated lime rind
1/2 cup lime juice
180g unsalted butter, chopped

For lime curd, whisk egg yolks, sugar and lime rind in the top of a double saucepan or in a heatproof bowl over simmering water until sugar dissolves and mixture is pale, then stir in lime juice and mix well. Add butter, piece by piece, stirring until each piece has melted. Continue to stir until mixture thickens enough to coat the back of a wooden spoon. Do not boil. Cool to room temperature, then place in a sterilised jar.

Process flour, icing sugar, coconut and butter in a food processor until mixture resembles breadcrumbs. Add egg and process until mixture just comes together. Turn out onto a lightly floured surface and knead until smooth. Shape into a disc, wrap in plastic wrap and refrigerate for 30 minutes. Cut dough in half and roll out between 2 sheets of baking paper until 3mm thick. Using a 5cm biscuit cutter, cut out rounds. Place rounds in 4cm patty pans, prick bases with a fork and bake at 180C for 10-12 minutes or until golden. Cool.

Place a spoonful of curd in tart shells, top each with 2 slices of mango and a raspberry and dust with icing sugar.

Makes 32 tarts.

simple asian dinner

SPICED CALAMARI ON LIME-CARROT SALAD

2 calamari hoods, cleaned and skinned
2 teaspoons sea salt
1 teaspoon black peppercorns
Pinch of chilli powder
1/2 teaspoon chinese five-spice powder
2 tablespoons peanut oil

LIME-CARROT SALAD

2 fresh, small red chillies,
    seeded and finely chopped
Grated rind and juice of 2 limes
2 tablespoons caster sugar
1 tablespoon sake
1 tablespoon white vinegar
1 tablespoon fish sauce
2 carrots, julienned
100g snowpeas, julienned
4 green onions, sliced on the diagonal
2 tablespoons coriander leaves
2 tablespoons thai basil leaves

For lime-carrot salad, combine chilli, lime rind and juice, sugar, sake, vinegar and fish sauce in a bowl and mix well. Combine carrot, snowpea, green onion and herbs, pour dressing over and toss to combine.

Run a knife down the side of calamari hoods and open out flat, then, using a sharp knife, score inside surface and cut each piece into 4. Combine salt, pepper, chilli powder and five-spice powder in a mortar and pestle and pound until a fine powder forms. Sprinkle spice mixture over calamari. Heat a wok over medium heat, add peanut oil and, when just beginning to smoke, add calamari and stir-fry over high heat until calamari curls and is just cooked. Divide salad among 4 plates and top with calamari.
wine: Wolf Blass Gold Label Riesling, SA.

THAI-STYLE RED BEEF CURRY

2 tablespoons peanut oil
500g sirloin steak, thinly sliced
1 onion, sliced lengthwise
2 tablespoons red-curry paste,
    or to taste
3 kaffir-lime leaves
1 2/3 cups coconut milk
2 tablespoons lime juice
3 teaspoons palm sugar
1 red capsicum, thinly sliced
1/2 bunch snake beans,
    cut into 5cm lengths
1/2 cup chopped coriander
Steamed jasmine rice, to serve

Heat 1 tablespoon peanut oil in a wok and cook beef, in batches, over high heat until browned. Remove meat from pan, then add remaining oil and onion to wok and stir-fry over high heat for 3 minutes. Add curry paste and cook for 2 minutes or until aromatic. Stir in 1/2 cup water and cook for 1 minute. Add kaffir-lime leaves, coconut milk, lime juice, sugar, capsicum and beans and simmer for 8 minutes. Add beef and coriander and simmer for another 3-5 minutes until heated through. Serve curry on a bed of steamed jasmine rice.
wine: Preece Merlot, Nagambie Lakes, Vic.

MASCARPONE MOUSSE WITH BANANAS AND PEANUT BRITTLE

2 eggs, separated
30g sugar
175g mascarpone
20ml dark rum
2 bananas, sliced

PEANUT BRITTLE

200g caster sugar
100g freshly roasted unsalted peanuts

For peanut brittle, combine sugar and 1/4 cup water in a small saucepan and stir over low heat until sugar dissolves. Bring to the boil and cook without stirring until golden. Spread peanuts over a baking-paper-lined oven tray and pour caramel over. Cool until hard, then break coarsely. Process two-thirds of the brittle in a food processor until coarse crumbs form.

Using an electric mixer, beat egg yolks and sugar until thick and pale, then gently fold in mascarpone and rum until just combined. Separately, beat egg whites until soft peaks form, then fold into mascarpone cream. Layer banana, ground peanut brittle and mascarpone cream in four 3/4-cup-capacity glasses and serve immediately, topped with remaining pieces of peanut brittle.
wine: Woodstock Botrytis Sweet White, McLaren Vale, SA.

Light and spicy
seafood on a
sharp—sweet salad,
a fragrant and very
easy curry, then
everyone is ready
for a cool, creamy
dessert with the
back-to-childhood
fun of homemade
peanut brittle.

greek buffet

menu serves 12

feta and cumin-seed fritters

yellow-split-pea dip

green-vegetable pie

roasted lamb with oregano, lemon and potatoes

tuna, tomato and olives with skordalia

cauliflower, celery and pickled red-onion salad

zucchini salad with mint

spinach and herb risoni

orange and cheese filo tart

strawberries in ouzo syrup with walnut shortbread pears

FETA AND CUMIN-SEED FRITTERS;
YELLOW-SPLIT-PEA DIP; GREEN-VEGETABLE PIE

time planner

in advance: keep in airtight container

• walnut shortbread pears can be made 1 week ahead

one day ahead: keep covered in refrigerator

• make yellow-split-pea dip, green-vegetable pie

and skordalia

• marinate lamb

on the day

• prepare tart shell, filling for tart, syrup and orange slices

• make zucchini and cauliflower salads

and spinach and herb risoni

• place lamb and potatoes on to cook

• marinate strawberries

• prepare and deep-fry feta and cumin-seed fritters

• serve fritters, dip and vegetable pie

• chop tomatoes and char-grill tuna

• serve tuna, lamb and accompaniments

• assemble tart and serve desserts

FETA AND CUMIN-SEED FRITTERS

150g Greek feta, crumbled
150g kasseri or cheddar,
    cut into 5mm pieces
150g kefalotiri or parmesan,
    cut into 5mm pieces
60g plain flour
2 teaspoons finely chopped thyme
2 teaspoons cumin seeds, roasted
2 eggs, lightly beaten
Light olive oil or vegetable oil,
    for deep-frying
Lemon wedges, to serve

Combine cheeses, flour, thyme, cumin and eggs in a bowl, season to taste and mix well. Heat oil in a large saucepan until hot and deep-fry tablespoonfuls of cheese mixture, in batches, for 2-3 minutes or until golden. Drain on absorbent paper, then transfer to a plate. Serve fritters immediately with lemon wedges.

Makes about 24.

YELLOW-SPLIT-PEA DIP

200g (1 cup) yellow split peas
1 small onion, coarsely chopped
4 cloves of garlic, flattened
1/3 cup extra virgin olive oil
1/4 cup lemon juice, or to taste
1 teaspoon ground cumin, roasted
1 teaspoon ground coriander, roasted
Warm pita bread, to serve

Place split peas in a saucepan, add enough cold water to just cover and bring to the boil. Drain and rinse. Return peas with onion and garlic to pan, add enough cold water to cover by 6cm and bring to the boil. Simmer over medium heat for 25 minutes or until peas are tender and beginning to collapse. Drain and cool to room temperature, then process in a food processor until smooth. With motor running, gradually add oil in a steady stream, then add 1/4 cup lemon juice, cumin and coriander and mix well. Season to taste, adding more lemon juice if necessary. Serve dip with warm pita bread.

Makes about 2 1/4 cups.

The sunny flavours and aromas of Greece – this
is relaxed, help-yourself food to be made ahead
of time and simply piled on plates. No need to
worry about keeping it hot or cold – Greek food
is perfect served warm or at room temperature.

GREEN-VEGETABLE PIE

260g zucchini (about 3), very thinly sliced
1 teaspoon salt
200g beans, trimmed
780g chicory (1 bunch)
    or silverbeet leaves,
    trimmed to 300g and chopped
125g Greek feta, crumbled
125g kefalotiri or parmesan, grated
1/4 cup chopped flat-leaf parsley
2 tablespoons chopped dill
1 tablespoon chopped mint
50g oven-dried breadcrumbs,
    finely processed
6 eggs, lightly beaten
35g (1/4 cup) sesame seeds,
    lightly roasted
Olive oil, for greasing

Combine zucchini and salt in a colander over a bowl and stand at room temperature for 30 minutes, then rinse zucchini under cold water and pat dry with absorbent paper. Add beans to a large saucepan of boiling, salted water and simmer for 5 minutes or until tender, then, using a slotted spoon, remove and plunge into a bowl of ice-cold water. Drain. Add chicory or silverbeet to remaining water in pan, bring water back to the boil, then drain immediately. Cool chicory or silverbeet under running water, then drain again. Squeeze chicory or silverbeet to remove excess moisture, then pat dry with absorbent paper and finely chop. Finely chop beans and place in a large bowl with chicory or silverbeet, add remaining ingredients, season to taste with cracked black pepper and mix well.

Spoon mixture into an oiled, base-lined 24cm springform pan and bake at 180C for 35-45 minutes or until mixture is set and top is golden. Stand pie in pan for 15 minutes before removing from tin. Cut into thin wedges and serve warm or at room temperature.

ROASTED LAMB WITH OREGANO, LEMON AND POTATOES

2 x 1.75-2kg easy-carve legs of lamb
1/4 cup lemon juice
1/2 cup olive oil
12 cloves of garlic, crushed
1/2 cup firmly packed
    oregano leaves, chopped
1 teaspoon flaked sea salt
1 teaspoon cracked black pepper
250ml dry white wine or water
1kg chat potatoes,
    washed and well dried
2 tablespoons torn
    oregano leaves, extra
1/4 cup finely chopped flat-leaf parsley

Place lamb in a large glass or ceramic dish and pour lemon juice over, turning lamb to coat.

Combine oil, garlic, oregano, sea salt and cracked black pepper in a small bowl and mix well. Using a spoon or your hand, push 1 tablespoon of garlic mixture into the centre of each lamb leg. Rub remaining garlic mixture all over lamb, cover and refrigerate for 24 hours.

Transfer lamb to 2 large roasting pans, spoon over any herb mixture and juice left in dish, then add white wine or water. Place lamb in a 210C oven, immediately reduce oven temperature to 170C and roast for 1 1/2 hours. Add potatoes and extra oregano to roasting pans, season to taste with flaked sea salt and cracked black pepper, then return to oven for 30-45 minutes or until lamb is tender and well browned. Remove lamb from roasting pans and rest in a warm place for 15 minutes.

Increase oven temperature to 210C, combine potatoes in 1 pan, return to the top shelf in the oven and roast for another 15 minutes or until tender and well browned. Transfer lamb to a large plate with potatoes. Serve potatoes sprinkled with parsley.

TUNA, TOMATO AND OLIVES WITH SKORDALIA

12 tuna steaks (about 150-200g each)
Extra virgin olive oil
800g vine-ripened tomatoes, chopped
1/4 cup torn basil leaves
150g large green olives,
    pitted and sliced

SKORDALIA
1 egg yolk
55g ground almonds
3 cloves of garlic, crushed
1/4 cup lemon juice
1 cup olive oil

For skordalia, process egg yolk, almonds and garlic in a food processor until well combined. Add lemon juice and process until combined, then with motor running gradually add olive oil and process until mixture is thick and creamy (if mixture is too thick, add a little cold water). Transfer sauce to a bowl and season to taste.

Season tuna steaks with sea salt and cracked black pepper, rub with a little extra virgin olive oil, then char-grill or barbecue, in batches, over high heat for 1-2 minutes on each side, depending on thickness of steaks.

Combine tomato, basil and olives on a large plate and sprinkle with sea salt and cracked black pepper to taste. Drizzle with extra virgin olive oil and top with char-grilled tuna steaks.

Serve tuna and tomato mixture warm or at room temperature with skordalia passed separately.

CAULIFLOWER,
CELERY AND PICKLED
RED-ONION SALAD

wines: Here are some suggestions
for what to drink with these dishes.
Orlando Trilogy Cuvée Brut, SA. The
name Trilogy acknowledges the blend of
the three varieties of classic Champagne
– chardonnay, pinot noir and pinot
meunier. Together, they produce a fresh
and flavoursome sparkling wine, a perfect
aperitif to go with Greek-inspired
mezes. Tulloch Hunter Valley Verdelho,
Hunter Valley, NSW. Verdelho is a wine
best enjoyed while still showing its
youthful freshness of ripe peaches,
rockmelon (cantaloupe) and tropical
fruits. Its zesty acidity adds to its ability
to pair perfectly with the savoury and
spicy ingredients of this buffet. Seppelt
Sunday Creek Pinot Noir, Vic. Pinot noir
has sweet strawberry and raspberry fruit
flavours, gentle tannins and a precise
acidity. It is perfectly capable of cutting
through the slight fattiness of the lamb,
yet it is subtle enough to combine well
with the tuna, tomato and olives.

CAULIFLOWER,
CELERY AND PICKLED
RED-ONION SALAD

1.6kg cauliflower, trimmed
   and cut into florets
Olive oil
6 sticks of celery, trimmed
   and sliced on the diagonal
1 1/2 tablespoons currants
1 large spanish onion,
   halved and thinly sliced
2 tablespoons white-wine vinegar
1 1/2 tablespoons caster sugar
100g large kalamata olives,
   pitted and quartered
50g (1/3 cup) pinenuts, roasted
1/4 cup lemon juice
2 tablespoons chopped oregano

Add cauliflower to a large saucepan of
boiling, salted water and cook over
medium heat until just tender. Drain and
refresh immediately in cold water, then
drain again and transfer to a large bowl.

Heat 2 tablespoons olive oil in a frying
pan, add celery and currants and cook
over medium heat for 5 minutes or until
tender, then add to cauliflower in bowl.

Combine onion, vinegar and sugar
in a small frying pan and stir over medium
heat for 5 minutes or until onion is soft.
Remove from heat, cover and cool to
room temperature, then add to cauliflower
mixture in bowl. Add remaining ingredients
and 2 tablespoons olive oil, season to
taste and toss gently.

ZUCCHINI SALAD
WITH MINT

Olive oil
1 large leek, white part only, chopped
600g small zucchini,
   cut lengthwise into 5mm-thick slices
600g small yellow zucchini,
   cut lengthwise into 5mm-thick slices
2 tablespoons white-wine vinegar
2 tablespoons chopped mint
2 tablespoons chopped flat-leaf parsley
1 tablespoon chopped coriander

Heat 1 tablespoon olive oil in a small
frying pan, add leek and cook over
medium heat for 10 minutes or until soft.

Brush zucchini lightly with olive oil,
season to taste, then grill, in batches,
under a hot grill until lightly browned
on both sides, or cook, in batches, in a
non-stick frying pan until browned on
both sides. Combine leek, zucchini and
remaining ingredients in a large bowl,
season to taste and toss gently.

SPINACH AND HERB RISONI

350g (1 3/4 cups) risoni
Olive oil
500g spinach (1 bunch),
   trimmed and washed
1/3 cup chopped dill
4 green onions, finely chopped
1/2 baby cos lettuce,
   trimmed and shredded
3/4 cup coarsely chopped
   flat-leaf parsley
2 tablespoons torn basil leaves
1/4 cup lemon juice

Cook pasta in a large saucepan of boiling,
salted water until al dente, then drain,
rinse under running water and drain again.
Transfer pasta to a large bowl, add 1/4 cup
olive oil and toss to combine.

Heat 2 tablespoons olive oil in a large,
heavy-based frying pan, add spinach and
toss over high heat until wilted, then drain.
Coarsely chop spinach and add to pasta
with remaining ingredients, season to taste
and mix well.

ORANGE AND CHEESE FILO TART

125ml red wine
125ml ruby port
110g (1/2 cup) caster sugar
2 bay leaves
3 strips of orange rind
6 oranges, peeled
    and cut into 1cm-thick slices
60g unsalted butter, melted
10 sheets of filo pastry

FILLING

100g soft, mild goat's cheese, crumbled
2 teaspoons grated orange rind
40g (1/4 cup) icing sugar
500g mascarpone

Combine wine, port, sugar, bay leaves and orange rind in a large, deep frying pan or a large, wide saucepan and stir over medium heat until sugar dissolves. Bring mixture to a simmer, add one third of the orange slices and poach gently for 2-3 minutes then, using a slotted spoon, remove slices from pan and drain on absorbent paper. Repeat the process with remaining orange slices, then simmer poaching liquid over high heat until reduced to a thick syrup, remove from heat and cool.

Brush a round 28cm tart tin with removable base with a little butter. Brush 1 sheet of filo with butter and place in tart tin. Brush another filo sheet with butter and place over the other to form a cross, repeating process with remaining filo sheets and butter. Trim pastry edge so that pastry extends 1cm over edge of tin. Line tart shell with baking paper, fill with dried beans or rice and bake blind at 180C for 20 minutes or until nearly dry and crisp. Remove paper and beans and bake for another 5 minutes or until pastry is dry and lightly cooked. If pastry rises in the centre, press down gently with a clean tea towel. Cool.

For filling, beat goat's cheese, orange rind and icing sugar until light and fluffy, then stir in mascarpone until just combined. Spoon filling into tart shell and top with orange slices, slightly overlapping. Brush top of tart with syrup and serve immediately.

STRAWBERRIES IN OUZO SYRUP WITH WALNUT SHORTBREAD PEARS

1kg strawberries, hulled and halved
40ml ouzo or sambuca
1/3 cup orange juice
2 tablespoons lime juice
80g (1/2 cup) icing sugar
Greek-style plain yoghurt, to serve

WALNUT SHORTBREAD PEARS

250g soft unsalted butter, chopped
160g (1 cup) icing sugar, sifted
1 teaspoon vanilla extract
1 egg yolk
20ml brandy or water
400g (2 2/3 cups) plain flour
1/2 teaspoon baking powder
110g walnuts,
    roasted and finely chopped
42 cloves
Icing sugar, extra, for dusting

For walnut shortbread pears, using an electric mixer, beat butter and icing sugar until just combined. Add vanilla, egg yolk and brandy or water and beat until just combined. On low speed, gradually beat in combined sifted flour and baking powder and walnuts until mixture just comes together. Form walnut-sized pieces of dough into pear shapes and place 6cm apart on baking-paper-lined oven trays. Holding stem, press a clove into the top of each shortbread, then cover shortbread and refrigerate for 30 minutes. Bake at 180C for 15-20 minutes or until light golden (shortbread will slump slightly). Cool shortbread on trays, then transfer to a large airtight container, storing shortbread in a single layer, and dust heavily with icing sugar.

Combine strawberries, ouzo and citrus juices in a large bowl, sift icing sugar over and toss gently to combine. Stand strawberries at room temperature for 30 minutes for icing sugar to dissolve and flavours to develop. Serve strawberries with walnut shortbread pears and yoghurt passed separately.

Makes about 42 shortbread.

lunch for friends

LEEK AND ARTICHOKE TART WITH POMEGRANATE-MOLASSES DRESSING

2 tablespoons extra virgin olive oil
2 leeks, white part only, sliced
200g rocket, trimmed
2 eggs
1/2 cup pouring cream
2 x 300g jars bottled whole
    artichoke hearts in brine (10-12),
    drained and halved
20g (1/4 cup) grated Parmigiano Reggiano
150g baby rocket

POMEGRANATE-MOLASSES DRESSING

1 tablespoon pomegranate molasses
1 tablespoon lemon juice
1/4 cup light olive oil

PASTRY

185g (1 1/4 cups) plain flour
40g (1/4 cup) polenta
100g cold unsalted butter, chopped
1 egg

For pomegranate-molasses dressing, combine all ingredients, season to taste and whisk well.

For pastry, process flour, polenta and 1/2 teaspoon salt in a food processor until well combined. Add butter and, using pulse button, pulse until mixture resembles fine breadcrumbs. Add egg and process until pastry just comes together, stopping the machine before the dough becomes a solid mass.

Gently knead dough on a lightly floured surface until smooth, then wrap in plastic wrap and refrigerate for 2 hours.

Roll out pastry on a lightly floured surface until 3mm thick and line a 2.5cm-deep, 10x34cm rectangular tart tin with removable base. Trim pastry so it extends 5mm above edge of tart tin. Cover and refrigerate for 1 hour. Line tart shell with baking paper, fill with dried beans or rice and bake blind at 190C for 10 minutes. Remove paper and beans and cook for another 10 minutes or until pastry is crisp and golden. Cool.

Heat olive oil in a frying pan, add leek and cook, covered, stirring occasionally, over low heat for 20 minutes or until leek is very soft.

Place rocket in a bowl and cover with boiling water, then drain immediately and plunge into iced water, then drain again. Squeeze excess moisture from rocket and chop very finely. Combine eggs, cream and chopped rocket, season to taste and mix well. Place artichoke halves, cut side down, on absorbent paper and stand for 5 minutes. Spread leek over base of tart, then place artichoke halves upright in 2 rows, pressing bases into leek. Pour egg mixture over (the mixture will not completely cover the artichokes) and sprinkle with parmesan.

Bake at 180C for 30 minutes or until just set, then transfer tart to a wire rack and stand in tart tin for 15 minutes before serving.

Combine baby rocket and 2 tablespoons dressing in a bowl and toss gently.

To serve, place slices of tart on 8 plates with baby rocket to one side, then drizzle plate with remaining dressing.

wine: Crochet Sancerre "Clos du Chene Marchand", Loire Valley, France. Both leeks and artichoke have intense vegetal flavours that require an equally intense wine with fresh, crisp, savoury fruit flavours. This Sancerre (made from sauvignon blanc) has subtle flavours of fresh gooseberries and custard apples and a delicious appley acid edge.

time planner

one day ahead: keep covered in refrigerator

• prepare pomegranate-molasses dressing
• bake tart shell: keep in airtight container
• make vanilla syrup and spice cake:
keep cake covered at room temperature

on the day

• prepare filling for tart, assemble and bake
• prepare saffron and tomato sauce
• serve tart with dressing
• cook pasta and moreton bay bugs and serve
• grill stone fruit and serve with cake and syrup

Familiar dishes – a savoury tart, then seafood
pasta – are lifted to simple elegance by luxury
vegetables and shellfish. The dessert cake
is lush but easy, and can be made well ahead.

LEEK AND ARTICHOKE TART WITH
POMEGRANATE-MOLASSES DRESSING

MORETON BAY BUGS WITH PAPPARDELLE,
SAFFRON AND TOMATO

MORETON BAY BUGS WITH PAPPARDELLE, SAFFRON AND TOMATO

Olive oil
1 onion, finely chopped
3 cloves of garlic, finely chopped
4 sticks of celery, finely chopped
3 bulbs of baby fennel,
    trimmed and finely chopped
1 tablespoon chopped thyme leaves
1 teaspoon grated orange rind
1 teaspoon (about 1g)
    firmly packed saffron threads
1/4 cup tomato paste
180ml dry white wine
8 very ripe vine-ripened tomatoes,
    peeled, seeded and chopped
600g dried pappardelle
600g moreton bay bug meat or 2.4kg
    uncooked moreton bay bugs, shelled

Heat 1/4 cup olive oil in a large heavy-based saucepan, add onion, garlic, celery, fennel, thyme and orange rind and cook over medium heat, stirring occasionally, for 10 minutes. Add saffron and tomato paste and cook for another 5 minutes. Add wine and cook until liquid has almost evaporated, then add 3 cups water and simmer gently for 15 minutes or until vegetables are tender. Add tomato and cook until heated through, then season to taste.

Meanwhile, add pasta to a large saucepan of boiling, salted water and boil for 5-6 minutes or until pasta is al dente, then drain. Transfer pasta to a large bowl, add sauce and toss gently to combine.

Heat a large frying pan until very hot, add 2 tablespoons olive oil and bug meat and toss over high heat for 2-3 minutes until meat is just tender.

Divide pasta mixture among 8 plates and top with bug meat.

wine: Domaine Tempier Bandol Rosé, Provence, France. Bug meat is one of the sweetest of all seafoods and saffron, a classic spice, adds a subtle piquancy to this recipe. Australian rosés tend to be overtly fruity, but those of Provence are light, dry and flavoursome. Their pale salmon-pink colour in no way reflects a lack of flavour intensity.

PISTACHIO SPICE CAKE WITH STONE FRUIT IN VANILLA SYRUP

6 eggs, separated
250g caster sugar
100g (2/3 cup) shelled pistachios,
    very finely ground
150g ground almonds
1 teaspoon ground coriander
35g (1/4 cup) self-raising flour
50g butter, melted
5 nectarines, halved and stoned
5 plums, halved and stoned
Icing sugar, for dusting

VANILLA SYRUP

55g (1/4 cup) caster sugar
2 tablespoons lemon juice
1 vanilla bean, split lengthwise
1 tablespoon Grenadine, optional

For vanilla syrup, combine sugar, lemon juice, scraped seeds of vanilla bean and bean, Grenadine, if using, and 1/2 cup water in a small saucepan and stir over medium heat until sugar dissolves, then bring to the boil. Reduce heat and simmer gently for 5 minutes until syrupy, then remove vanilla bean.

Using an electric mixer, beat egg yolks and half the sugar on high speed for 5 minutes or until mixture is pale and very thick. Transfer to a large bowl, stir in ground nuts, coriander, flour and butter and mix well. Separately, beat egg whites until soft peaks form, then gradually add remaining sugar and beat until firm peaks form. Using a large metal spoon, mix half the egg-white mixture into nut mixture until combined, then gently fold in remaining egg-white mixture until incorporated. Spoon mixture into a greased, base-lined 24cm springform pan, smooth top and bake at 180C, covering with foil if necessary to prevent from overbrowning, for 45 minutes or until cooked when tested with a skewer. Stand cake in pan for 5 minutes before turning out on a wire rack to cool (the base will become the top).

Place fruit in a single layer on a baking tray, brush with 1/4 cup vanilla syrup and grill under a hot grill for 5-7 minutes or until fruit is warm and beginning to brown around edges.

Dust cake with icing sugar and serve wedges with grilled fruit drizzled with remaining vanilla syrup.

wine: Domaine Bourillon-d'Orléans Vouvray Demi Sec, Loire Valley, France. Vouvray is made from chenin blanc, a variety rarely exciting when grown in Australia. This one is only semi-sweet, yet there is enough richness to match the nuttiness of the cake and the piercing acidity parries the intense flavours of the stone fruits.

simple vegetarian lunch

menu serves 4

bruschetta with pumpkin, gorgonzola and sage

salsa agresto with penne, asparagus and butter beans

baked figs with raspberries

BRUSCHETTA WITH PUMPKIN, GORGONZOLA AND SAGE

1.2kg butternut pumpkin, peeled,
    seeded and cut into 1cm pieces
1 tablespoon sage leaves, torn
Extra virgin olive oil
8 thick slices of sourdough
1 clove of garlic, flattened
120g gorgonzola or another strong
    blue-vein cheese, sliced into 8

Place pumpkin and sage leaves in a large roasting pan, drizzle with 2 tablespoons olive oil, season to taste and toss to coat. Roast at 220C for 15-20 minutes or until pumpkin is soft and beginning to brown around edges.

Toast bread on both sides until golden, then rub with garlic and brush with 2 tablespoons oil. Divide pumpkin and sage among toasted slices and top with cheese. Place on an oven tray and bake at 180C for 5-10 minutes or until cheese just begins to melt and pumpkin is hot. Serve drizzled with a little more oil and sprinkled with cracked black pepper.
wine: Lindemans Hunter Valley Semillon, Hunter Valley, NSW.

SALSA AGRESTO WITH PENNE, ASPARAGUS AND BUTTER BEANS

60g (1/2 cup) chopped, roasted walnuts
80g (1/2 cup) chopped,
    dry-roasted almonds
1 cup loosely packed basil leaves
1 cup loosely packed
    flat-leaf parsley leaves
1/2 cup olive oil
1/4 cup verjuice
250g asparagus, chopped
300g butter beans, sliced lengthwise
400g dried penne
2 tablespoons basil leaves, extra, torn

Process walnuts, almonds, basil and parsley in a food processor until finely chopped. With motor running, add combined oil and verjuice and process until a coarse paste forms. Season to taste.

Steam asparagus and butter beans together until just tender.

Cook pasta in a large saucepan of boiling, salted water for 7-10 minutes or until al dente, then drain. Return pasta to same saucepan, add three-quarters of the salsa and extra basil leaves and toss well. Divide pasta mixture among 4 shallow bowls and top with vegetables and remaining salsa.
wine: Tahbilk Marsanne, Nagambie Lakes, Vic.

BAKED FIGS WITH RASPBERRIES

50g butter, chopped
100ml dry white wine
2 tablespoons brown sugar
2 bay leaves
8 figs
250g raspberries
Crème fraîche, to serve

Combine butter, wine, sugar and bay leaves in a saucepan and simmer over low heat until sugar dissolves. Increase heat and boil until reduced by one third. Halve figs, place in an ovenproof dish to fit snugly and pour wine mixture over. Bake at 180C for 10 minutes or until figs are tender. Remove from oven, add raspberries to dish and cool figs slightly. Serve in 4 bowls, with crème fraîche passed separately.
wine: Heggies Vineyard Botrytis Riesling, Eden Valley, SA.

Make this vegetarian menu for an easy lunch, or
remember the bruschetta or the pasta when you
want something simple but inspired for supper.

summer brunch

BLOODY MARY

time planner

in advance

● cinnamon dressing can be made 1 week ahead:

keep covered in refrigerator

● bases for semolina and cardamom galettes can be made

5 days ahead: keep in airtight container

one day ahead: keep covered in refrigerator

● poach peaches, add lychees

● cook saffron-onion confit, blanch sausages

on the day

● make preserved-lemon and chervil dressing

● prepare couscous, rocket salad

● roast tomatoes and eggplant, process ricotta and goat's cheese

● barbecue sausages

● cook figs and assemble galettes

● pan-fry turkish bread and top with goat's-cheese mixture

and roasted vegetables

● make bloody mary and serve

● assemble all dishes and serve together

BLOODY MARY

400ml vodka
1 litre chilled tomato juice
1/3 cup lemon juice, or to taste
Dash of worcestershire sauce
Dash of Tabasco, to serve
Ice cubes and 10 small sticks of celery,
    green leaves still attached, to serve

Combine vodka and tomato juice in a large jug, add lemon juice, worcestershire sauce and Tabasco to taste and mix well, then season to taste. Place ice cubes and celery sticks in 10 highball glasses, pour in bloody mary and serve.

PEACHES AND LYCHEES IN ROSEWATER SYRUP WITH THICK YOGHURT AND PISTACHIOS

8g (1/3 cup) dried rose petals
750ml sparkling white wine
440g (2 cups) caster sugar
Zested rind and juice of 2 oranges
2 cloves
1/2 vanilla bean, split lengthwise
20 small just-ripe peaches
30 lychees (about 900g),
    peeled and seeded
1kg Greek-style plain yoghurt,
    drained overnight in a sieve
    lined with damp muslin
50g (1/3 cup) shelled pistachios, halved

Place rose petals in a small piece of muslin and tie with kitchen string. Place muslin bag, wine, sugar, orange rind and juice, cloves and vanilla bean in a large saucepan and stir over medium heat until sugar dissolves, then bring to the boil. Add half the peaches, cover and simmer over low heat for 10-15 minutes or until peaches are just tender. Using a slotted spoon, remove peaches from syrup and transfer to a large bowl. Repeat with remaining peaches and poaching liquid. Cool peaches to room temperature, then peel away skin. Add lychees to the same bowl.

Simmer poaching liquid over medium heat until reduced to 2 cups and syrupy, then remove muslin bag, cloves and vanilla bean. Pour hot syrup over fruits and cool to room temperature or refrigerate for up to 1 day.

Serve peaches and lychees with thick yoghurt sprinkled with pistachios.

This could be a super breakfast for a crowd or a late-morning brunch that drifts into lunch, in which case you might want to move the rosewater fruits and fig galettes to the end of proceedings and call them dessert.

PEACHES AND LYCHEES IN ROSEWATER SYRUP
WITH THICK YOGHURT AND PISTACHIOS

SEMOLINA AND CARDAMOM GALETTES WITH FRESH FIGS

200g (1 cup, firmly packed)
    light brown sugar
15 black figs, halved
Thick cream, to serve

SEMOLINA AND CARDAMOM GALETTES

250g fine semolina
110g (1/2 cup) caster sugar
100g ground almonds
1/2 teaspoon ground cinnamon
1/2 teaspoon ground cardamom
150g butter, chopped
1 egg

For semolina and cardamom galettes, process semolina, sugar, almonds, spices and butter in a food processor until mixture resembles coarse breadcrumbs. Add egg and process until mixture comes together in a ball. Roll 2-level-tablespoon quantities of dough into balls and refrigerate for 30 minutes or until dough is firm. Roll out balls on a floured surface until 10cm round, place on baking-paper-lined oven trays and bake at 180C for 10-15 minutes or until crisp and golden. Cool on trays.

Spread brown sugar over base of a non-stick frying pan and cook over low heat for 2 minutes until warm, then add 1/4 cup boiling water and stir until sugar dissolves. Increase heat and bring mixture to a simmer. Add half the figs, cut side down, and cook on both sides for 1-2 minutes or until warmed. Transfer figs to a plate. Repeat with remaining figs.

Top 10 galettes with 3 fig halves each and a dollop of thick cream, then drizzle a little sugar syrup over the top.

Makes 10.

SMOKED TROUT WITH PRESERVED-LEMON AND CHERVIL DRESSING

4 smoked trout (about 200g each)
Witlof, leaves separated,
    and watercress sprigs, to serve

PRESERVED-LEMON AND CHERVIL DRESSING

2-3 wedges of preserved lemon
1 cup olive oil
1/2 cup verjuice
1/3 cup chopped chervil
Pinch of caster sugar

Cut through skin on both sides of trout at head and tail and peel away skin.

For preserved-lemon and chervil dressing, remove and discard flesh from preserved-lemon wedges. Rinse rind and finely chop to give 2 tablespoons of chopped lemon. Process lemon with remaining ingredients in a food processor until well combined, then season to taste.

Serve trout with witlof and watercress and drizzle dressing over.

MERGUEZ SAUSAGES WITH SAFFRON-ONION CONFIT

20 merguez sausages (about 1.5kg)
Pinch of saffron threads, or to taste
1/2 tablespoon white-wine vinegar
1/4 cup extra virgin olive oil
6 spanish onions,
    halved and thinly sliced
2 teaspoons ras el hanout
1 tablespoon honey
Lemon wedges, to serve

Gently twist sausages in the middle to divide or tie in the middle with a piece of kitchen string. Place sausages in a large saucepan and add enough cold water to cover by 5cm. Bring water to the boil and cook over medium heat for 10-15 minutes or until sausages are cooked through. Drain and rinse under cold water, then pat dry with absorbent paper. Using scissors, cut sausages at twist or remove string and cut.

Combine saffron and vinegar in a small cup and stand for 5 minutes. Heat oil in a large, heavy-based saucepan, add onion and ras el hanout and stir over medium heat for 5 minutes until onion begins to soften. Add saffron mixture, reduce heat and cook, covered, stirring occasionally, for 45 minutes or until onion is very soft. Stir in honey and cook for another 5 minutes, then season to taste.

Barbecue sausages on a hot barbecue or grill under a hot grill until well browned and heated through.

Serve sausages and saffron-onion confit either warm or at room temperature with lemon wedges.

PAN-FRIED TURKISH BREAD WITH TOMATO, EGGPLANT AND GOAT'S CHEESE

10 vine-ripened tomatoes
    (about 1.25kg), halved
10 japanese eggplant (about 600g),
    halved lengthwise
2 teaspoons cumin seeds,
    roasted and crushed
2 teaspoons coriander seeds,
    roasted and crushed
2 fresh, small red chillies,
    seeded and finely chopped
Light olive oil
300g ricotta
125g soft, mild goat's cheese
5 eggs
1/2 cup milk
1 turkish bread loaf, split lengthwise
    and cut into 10 pieces
10 large mint leaves

Place tomato and eggplant, cut side up, in separate roasting pans and sprinkle both with combined spices and chilli, then drizzle with a little light olive oil and season to taste. Roast at 160C for 30 minutes, then swap pans from top to bottom and roast for another 30 minutes.

Process ricotta and goat's cheese in a food processor until smooth, then season to taste.

Whisk eggs and milk in a bowl, then slowly dip bread slices into egg mixture, allowing each to absorb some egg mixture. Heat 1 tablespoon light olive oil in a large, heavy-based frying pan and cook bread, in batches, over medium heat until browned on both sides, adding more oil as necessary.

Place bread on a large plate and top each slice with a little goat's-cheese mixture, 2 pieces of eggplant, 2 tomato halves and a mint leaf.

PAN-FRIED TURKISH BREAD
WITH TOMATO, EGGPLANT
AND GOAT'S CHEESE

DATE AND ALMOND COUSCOUS

800ml chicken or vegetable stock
    (see basic recipes)
1 cinnamon stick
800g (4 cups) couscous
120g butter, chopped
160g (1 cup) blanched almonds
220g (1 cup) fresh dates,
    seeded and sliced
1 cup flat-leaf parsley,
    coarsely chopped

Combine chicken or vegetable stock and cinnamon stick in a large saucepan and bring to the boil. Remove from heat, add couscous, then cover and stand for 10 minutes or until stock is absorbed. Remove cinnamon stick and fluff couscous with a fork to separate grains.

Heat 40g butter in a large, non-stick frying pan or wok until foamy, add almonds and cook over medium heat for 3-5 minutes or until almonds are golden. Using a slotted spoon, remove almonds. Add another 40g butter and half the couscous to butter in pan and cook couscous, tossing with a wooden spoon over medium heat for 5 minutes or until golden. Transfer to a large bowl, then repeat with remaining butter and couscous. Add almonds, dates and parsley to couscous, season to taste and mix well.

ROCKET AND ORANGE SALAD WITH CINNAMON DRESSING

200g baby rocket leaves
200g baby spinach leaves
4 oranges, peeled and thinly sliced

CINNAMON DRESSING

1/2 cup light olive oil
2 cinnamon sticks, crumbled
Zested rind of 1 orange
1/2 cup verjuice or white-wine vinegar

For cinnamon dressing, combine oil, cinnamon sticks and orange rind in a small frying pan and cook over low heat for 2 minutes until orange rind begins to sizzle. Remove from heat and stand at room temperature for 20 minutes. Strain oil, whisk in verjuice or vinegar and season to taste.

Combine salad leaves and orange slices in a large bowl, add dressing to taste and toss to combine.

Makes 1 cup dressing.

wines: Here are some suggestions for what to drink with these dishes. **Bimbadgen Estate Semillon, Hunter Valley, NSW.** The spices used in North African and Middle Eastern cooking are more savoury than the sweet spices of Asian cuisines. The crisp, fresh and herbal characters of semillon work best with these more savoury spices. Although its semillon vines are fully mature, Bimbadgen is a new label. **Brown Brothers Everton, Milawa, Vic.** A bold, tannic red would fight the strong spices in merguez sausages. The Everton red is blended to give soft savoury fruit flavours (black cherries and damson plums) with low tannins and minimal oak influence. An easy-drinking red. **Seppelt Botrytis Gewürztraminer, Eden Valley, SA.** The fruit flavours of gewürztraminer are often described as being like lychees, so what better to go with this peach and lychee combination than a wine made from gewürztraminer?

SMOKED TROUT WITH PRESERVED-LEMON
AND CHERVIL DRESSING; DATE AND
ALMOND COUSCOUS; MERGUEZ SAUSAGES
WITH SAFFRON-ONION CONFIT

simple dinner party

MARINATED LEEKS WITH PRAWNS AND FETA

8 small leeks, white part only,
   cut in half crosswise and lengthwise
1/4 cup olive oil
1/2 cup flat-leaf parsley leaves
500g cooked prawns, peeled
   and deveined, leaving tails intact
100g marinated feta, crumbled

MARINADE
1/4 cup extra virgin olive oil
2 tablespoons lemon juice
35g (1/4 cup) currants,
   soaked in boiling water for
   5 minutes, then drained

Place leek in a glass or ceramic ovenproof dish, drizzle with oil and turn to coat well. Season to taste and roast at 180C for 30 minutes, turning once.

For marinade, combine all ingredients and season to taste.

Scatter leek with parsley, pour marinade over, season to taste and mix gently. Cover and stand for 2-3 hours at room temperature. Serve leek mixture topped with prawns and feta.

wine: Brokenwood Cricket Pitch Sauvignon Blanc Semillon, NSW.

BAKED LAMB TOPSIDE WITH ROASTED RATATOUILLE AND GREEN SAUCE

2 lamb topsides (about 400g each)
1kg small pink-eye
   or desirée potatoes, halved
Olive oil
1 small eggplant, chopped
1 small onion, finely chopped
1 small zucchini, chopped
1 red capsicum, chopped
1 tomato, coarsely chopped
1 clove of garlic, chopped
1 tablespoon chopped flat-leaf parsley
1 tablespoon chopped thyme

GREEN SAUCE
1 1/2 cups basil leaves
1/2 cup mint leaves
1 clove of garlic, sliced
3/4 cup olive oil

For green sauce, process basil, mint and garlic in a food processor until finely chopped. With motor running, gradually add oil until a thin paste forms. Season to taste.

Place lamb and potato, cut side up, in a roasting pan, drizzle with oil and season to taste.

Combine eggplant, onion, zucchini, capsicum and tomato in another roasting pan, scatter with garlic and herbs, season to taste and drizzle with oil. Place lamb topsides on upper rack in oven and vegetables on lower rack and cook at 190C, stirring ratatouille occasionally, for 40 minutes. Remove lamb from roasting pan, cover with foil and rest in a warm place for 10 minutes. Continue cooking potatoes and vegetables until potatoes are golden and vegetables are tender.

Serve thinly sliced lamb with potatoes, roasted ratatouille and green sauce.

wine: Mildara Jamiesons Run Coonawarra Dry Red, Coonawarra, SA.

PLUM, WALNUT AND PINENUT TARTS

100g mascarpone
1 egg yolk
1/2 teaspoon ground cinnamon
55g (1/4 cup) caster sugar
2 sheets of ready-rolled
   butter puff pastry, halved
40g (1/3 cup) chopped walnuts, roasted
6 plums, halved, stoned and thinly sliced
2 tablespoons pinenuts, roasted
Thick cream, to serve

Combine mascarpone, egg yolk, cinnamon and 1 tablespoon sugar and mix well. Place pastry pieces 5cm apart on oven trays, spread each with mascarpone mixture, leaving a 3cm border all around. Sprinkle mascarpone with walnuts, then top with overlapping slices of plum. Sprinkle with pinenuts and fold in borders to partially cover topping. Bake at 220C for 12-15 minutes or until pastry is puffed and golden. Sprinkle hot pastries with remaining caster sugar and serve with thick cream.

wine: Seppelt Seppeltsfield Show Oloroso DP38, Barossa Valley, SA.

A dinner full of favourite treats – prawns, roast lamb and rich pastries. Like many of the first courses in this book, this savoury way to serve prawns is also an idea for a rather special lunch or supper.

MARINATED LEEKS WITH PRAWNS AND FETA

formal lunch

time planner

in advance

● ice-cream and wafers can be made 3 days ahead:

keep ice-cream in freezer and wafers in airtight container

one day ahead: keep covered in refrigerator

● make gazpacho and basil oil

● prepare dill and mustard mayonnaise

● prepare red-wine syrup

on the day

● poach trout, cook potatoes

● serve gazpacho

● transfer ice-cream to refrigerator

● prepare salad and serve trout and potatoes

● serve ice-cream and wafers with berries and syrup

ROASTED-TOMATO GAZPACHO WITH BASIL OIL

3kg vine-ripened tomatoes,
  halved and seeded
8 cloves of garlic, unpeeled
1/3 cup extra virgin olive oil
2 cups verjuice
Tomato juice or water, optional
1 sourdough loaf, crusts removed
  and bread cut into 1cm cubes
1/3 cup olive oil

SALSA
2 small lebanese cucumbers,
  finely chopped
1 spanish onion, finely chopped
1 small red capsicum, finely chopped
1 tablespoon aged red-wine vinegar

BASIL OIL
2 cups firmly packed basil leaves
200ml olive oil

Combine tomato and garlic in a large roasting pan, drizzle with extra virgin olive oil and roast at 200C for 1 hour. Cool. Process tomato and peeled garlic cloves with cooking juices in a food processor until smooth. Transfer to a bowl, add verjuice, season to taste with sea salt and cracked black pepper and mix well. Adjust consistency of soup, if necessary, with a little tomato juice or water. Refrigerate for 6 hours or overnight for flavours to develop.

Combine bread and olive oil in a baking dish and toss to coat. Bake at 200C for 15 minutes or until golden, turning occasionally.

For salsa, combine all ingredients, season to taste and mix well.

For basil oil, process basil in a food processor until finely chopped. With motor running, gradually add olive oil and process until well combined and smooth.

Serve chilled soup topped with salsa and croûtons and drizzled with basil oil.

wine: Emilio Lustau "Los Arcos" Amontillado, Jerez, Spain. Soup and sherry is a very traditional combination which is now, sadly, often overlooked. This amontillado shows a degree of richness, yet it also has a dry finish. It goes perfectly with the high acid content of this tomato-based soup, a classic dish from Spain, the home of sherry.

When you have an important celebration to cook for in hot weather, think of this lovely menu. It's classic, spectacular and, since everything except the potatoes is cold, you can prepare it in easy stages.

POACHED WHOLE OCEAN
TROUT WITH DILL AND
MUSTARD MAYONNAISE AND
MIXED-PEA AND BEAN SALAD

POACHED WHOLE OCEAN TROUT WITH DILL AND MUSTARD MAYONNAISE

1 x 2.5kg whole ocean trout,
    cleaned and scaled
1 small onion, sliced
2 bay leaves
6 sprigs of parsley
6 black peppercorns
1/4 cup white-wine vinegar
Mixed-pea and bean salad
    (recipe follows), to serve
1 1/2 cups dill and mustard mayonnaise
    (see basic recipes)
Steamed baby potatoes, to serve

Place fish in a poaching kettle, cover with cold water and add onion, bay leaves, parsley, peppercorns and vinegar. Cover and bring very slowly to the boil. As soon as water begins to boil, remove kettle from heat and remove lid. Leave fish to cook in liquid as it cools, turning once. Fish is cooked when dorsal fin comes out easily when pulled. (A 2.5kg fish will take about 2 hours to cook once heat has been turned off.)

Remove fish from poaching liquid. Carefully remove skin, leaving head and tail intact.

To serve, place mixed-bean and pea salad in the centre of 10 plates, top with a piece of trout and drizzle with dill and mustard mayonnaise. Or place whole trout on a large plate, spoon mixed-pea and bean salad around and pass dill and mustard mayonnaise separately. Serve with steamed baby potatoes.

MIXED-PEA AND BEAN SALAD

300g broad beans, podded to give 125g,
    steamed until tender, then peeled
200g snowpeas, blanched
    in boiling water for 10 seconds
200g sugarsnap peas, blanched
    in boiling water for 10 seconds
300g peas, podded to give
    120g and steamed until just tender
125g snowpea tendrils
75g snowpea sprouts
2 tablespoons olive oil
1 tablespoon verjuice

Combine broad beans, snowpeas, sugarsnaps, peas, tendrils and sprouts in a bowl, toss with olive oil and verjuice and season to taste.

wine: Domaine Champy Savigny les Beaune premier cru, Burgundy, France. Forget the old adage about drinking white wine with fish – this dish needs a flavoursome but not robust red, a role pinot noir plays perfectly. This Savigny les Beaune has sweet red berry and cherry flavours and a refreshing acidity, delivering both flavour and delicacy.

VANILLA-BEAN ICE-CREAM SANDWICH WITH BERRIES AND RED-WINE SYRUP

2 vanilla beans, split lengthwise
1½ cups milk
600ml pouring cream
7 egg yolks
130g caster sugar
1 teaspoon vanilla extract
1kg mixed berries (including
    strawberries, raspberries,
    blueberries) and cherries, to serve

WAFERS

100g soft unsalted butter, chopped
165g (¾ cup) caster sugar
¼ cup honey
75g (½ cup) plain flour
2 egg whites

RED-WINE SYRUP

250g sugar
750ml valpolicella
1 vanilla bean, split lengthwise

Scrape seeds of vanilla bean into milk. Combine milk, vanilla beans and cream in a saucepan and bring just to the boil.

Whisk egg yolks and sugar until thick and pale, then whisk in milk mixture. Pour mixture into a clean saucepan and stir continually with a wooden spoon over low heat until mixture thickens enough to coat the back of the spoon. Do not boil. Remove from heat, cover closely with plastic wrap and cool to room temperature. Remove vanilla beans and stir in vanilla extract.

Freeze in an ice-cream maker according to manufacturer's instructions, then store in a plastic-wrap-lined loaf tin or airtight container in the freezer.

For wafers, process butter, sugar, honey, flour and egg whites in a food processor until well combined and smooth. Spread mixture very thinly over 4 baking-paper-lined oven trays and bake at 180C for 10-15 minutes until well browned and cooked through. Cool on trays, then break into irregular-shaped wafers.

For red-wine syrup, combine sugar and 2 tablespoons water in a heavy-based saucepan and cook over low heat until sugar dissolves. Increase heat and cook syrup, without stirring, until it turns a rich caramel colour. Remove from heat, carefully add wine and vanilla bean, then bring to the boil and boil until reduced by half. Cool and remove vanilla bean.

Transfer ice-cream from freezer to refrigerator 15 minutes before serving. Turn out ice-cream, remove plastic wrap and cut ice-cream into 1.5cm-thick slices. Place a wafer on each plate, top with a slice of ice-cream, then another wafer, and serve with mixed berries and cherries drizzled with red-wine syrup.

wine: Château Climens premier cru, Sauternes, France. The dessert wines of Bordeaux offer a wonderful balance of fruit flavours, subtlety and complexity which enable them to match many desserts perfectly. This Château Climens is a stylish and luscious gem, with intense pear and apricot flavours and a fine acid which cuts the finish of the wine and the richness of this dessert.

VANILLA-BEAN ICE-CREAM SANDWICH
WITH BERRIES AND RED-WINE SYRUP

lazy summer picnic

VEGETABLE-FILLED ITALIAN LOAF

time planner

one day ahead: keep covered in refrigerator

• make salsa rossa and preserved-lemon and mint marinade

• prepare vegetables and fill loaf

• bake sweet basil ricotta

• prepare cardamom syrup, if using

on the day

• prepare vegetables and bake tart

• marinate blue eye

• cook beans, make hazelnut and red-capsicum dressing

• char-grill fish (or barbecue at picnic)

• assemble all dishes, transport to picnic and serve

POTATO, ANCHOVY AND ROCKET TART WITH SALSA ROSSA

40g butter, chopped
Olive oil
2 onions, finely chopped
6 anchovy fillets in olive oil,
    drained and finely chopped
2 tablespoons rosemary leaves
4 small pontiac potatoes, scrubbed
1 x 375g packet puff pastry
1 bunch rocket, trimmed
1 egg, lightly beaten

SALSA ROSSA

2 ripe egg tomatoes,
    seeded and finely chopped
2 red capsicum, roasted and peeled
    (see basic recipes)
1 small spanish onion, finely chopped
1 tablespoon torn basil leaves
2 tablespoons chervil leaves
1/4 cup extra virgin olive oil
2 tablespoons lemon juice

Heat butter and 1 tablespoon olive oil in a frying pan, add onion, anchovy and half the rosemary and stir occasionally over medium heat for 15 minutes or until onion is soft and golden. Cool.

Cook whole unpeeled potatoes in boiling, salted water until tender. Cool, then cut into 5mm-thick slices.

Roll out pastry on a lightly floured surface until 28x50cm in size and place on a large, greased oven tray. Spread pastry with onion mixture, leaving a 5cm border, then top with rocket and sliced potato. Fold the pastry border over potato to form a rim, leaving potato exposed in the centre. Brush rim with beaten egg, then sprinkle potato with remaining rosemary, drizzle with a little olive oil and season to taste. Bake at 220C for 15-20 minutes or until pastry is golden and puffed.

For salsa rossa, combine all ingredients, season to taste and mix well.

Serve tart warm or at room temperature with salsa rossa.

This menu in its entirety will serve eight picnickers, but remember the separate dishes for relaxed, 'pick-up' family meals by the pool, in the garden or on the veranda.

SWEET BASIL RICOTTA
WITH BERRIES AND PEACHES

.UE-EYE KEBABS WITH
RESERVED-LEMON AND
NT MARINADE; BEAN
ALAD WITH HAZELNUT
ND RED-CAPSICUM
RESSING

BEAN SALAD WITH HAZELNUT AND RED-CAPSICUM DRESSING

500g beans, trimmed
500g roman beans, trimmed
30g (1/4 cup) coarsely chopped
    hazelnuts, roasted, to serve

HAZELNUT AND RED-CAPSICUM DRESSING

1/2 cup extra virgin olive oil
1 small onion, thinly sliced
1 clove of garlic, finely chopped
1 fresh, small red chilli, finely chopped
2 egg tomatoes, chopped
1 red capsicum, roasted and peeled
    (see basic recipes), chopped
30g (1/4 cup) coarsely chopped
    hazlenuts, roasted
2 tablespoons lemon juice
15g (1/4 cup) fresh white breadcrumbs

For hazelnut and red-capsicum dressing, heat 1 tablespoon olive oil in a frying pan, add onion and cook over medium heat for 5 minutes. Add garlic, chilli, tomato and capsicum and cook for 10 minutes or until mixture is pulpy. Process tomato mixture with remaining olive oil, hazelnuts, lemon juice and breadcrumbs in a food processor until smooth. Season to taste.

Cook beans and roman beans separately in boiling, salted water until just tender, drain and refresh in ice-cold water, then drain again.

Place beans in a large bowl, add hazelnut and red-capsicum dressing and toss well to combine. Serve sprinkled with hazelnuts.

BLUE-EYE KEBABS WITH PRESERVED-LEMON AND MINT MARINADE

1.6kg blue-eye fillets, cut into
    30 pieces 3-4cm in size
40 fresh bay leaves
20 water-soaked bamboo skewers
Lemon wedges, to serve

PRESERVED-LEMON AND MINT MARINADE

1/3 cup chopped, rinsed
    preserved-lemon rind
1/2 cup mint leaves
4 cloves of garlic, crushed
2/3 cup extra virgin olive oil

For preserved-lemon and mint marinade, process all ingredients in a food processor until smooth, then transfer to a large bowl. Add blue eye, season generously with cracked black pepper and toss.

Drain blue eye, then thread onto skewers, alternating with bay leaves, and brush with marinade. Char-grill or barbecue, in batches, until just tender. Serve kebabs with lemon wedges.

VEGETABLE-FILLED ITALIAN LOAF

Olive oil
1 spanish onion, halved and thinly sliced
1 eggplant, cut into 5mm-thick slices
3 small zucchini (about 320g), cut
    lengthwise into 5mm-thick slices
1 x 20cm round Italian-style bread loaf
150g pesto (see basic recipes)
200g bocconcini, thinly sliced
20g baby spinach leaves, trimmed
2 tablespoons green- or black-olive
    tapenade (see basic recipes)
2 red capsicum, roasted and peeled
    (see basic recipes)

Heat 1 tablespoon olive oil in a frying pan, add onion and cook over medium heat for 10 minutes or until onion is soft.

Brush eggplant and zucchini with olive oil, place on oven trays and season to taste, then cook under a hot grill until lightly browned on both sides.

Using a serrated knife, cut top from loaf and reserve. Hollow out loaf, leaving a 1cm shell of bread, then brush cavity and underside of reserved lid with pesto.

Place eggplant, zucchini, bocconcini, spinach, onion, tapenade and capsicum in layers inside loaf, then replace lid. Wrap in plastic wrap and place on a tray, cover with another tray and weigh down with several cans of food. Refrigerate for 8 hours or overnight. Serve loaf cut into wedges.

SWEET BASIL RICOTTA WITH BERRIES AND PEACHES

1kg whole-milk ricotta, drained
200g icing sugar
3 eggs
15-20 small basil leaves
600g mixed berries in season,
    such as raspberries, strawberries
    and blueberries
4 peaches, halved,
    stoned and thickly sliced
Cardamom syrup (see basic recipes),
    optional, to serve

Whisk ricotta, icing sugar and eggs in a bowl until smooth. Spoon half the mixture into a greased and lined round 20cm cake tin and top with basil leaves in a single layer. Add remaining ricotta mixture and smooth top.

Place cake tin in a roasting pan and add enough boiling water to come halfway up side of tin, then bake at 150C for 30 minutes or until just set. Remove tin from bain-marie and grill under a hot grill until top browns. Cool to room temperature, then refrigerate overnight.

Remove baked ricotta from tin and serve wedges with berries and peaches drizzled with cardamom syrup, if using.

wines: Here are some suggestions for what to drink with these dishes. **Grant Burge Zerk Semillon, Barossa Valley, SA.** The Hunter Valley is known as the best site for semillon in Australia. As a result, the success of South Australia's semillon can be overlooked, but this Burge is a consistent performer at the wine shows and on the table. **Hardy Padthaway Unwooded Chardonnay, Padthaway, SA.** Many unwooded chardonnays lack depth and structure, but not this delightful wine from Hardy's vast Padthaway vineyards. It exhibits ripe tropical fruit flavours, a refreshing acidity and a smooth harmonious mouthfeel. **Howard Park Madfish Bay Premium Red, Great Southern, WA.** Australian red wines tend to be full-bodied and powerful, so powerful that often they can dominate lightly flavoured food. This Madfish Bay, with soft, plummy flavours and a light tannin structure, is a perfect picnic red. **Lillypilly Estate Botrytis Riesling, Riverina, NSW.** Most botrytised wines from the Riverina are made from semillon, but here riesling is used to make a more subtle and fruit-driven dessert wine without excessive botrytis or oak influence.

menus for cool weather

classic dinner party

PROSCIUTTO-WRAPPED BABY BOCCONCINI ON CROUTONS

PROSCIUTTO-WRAPPED BABY BOCCONCINI ON CROUTONS

1 1/2 teaspoons balsamic vinegar
Extra virgin olive oil
2 teaspoons thyme leaves
16 baby bocconcini
8 slices of prosciutto, each cut into 2
1/2 baguette, cut into 16 thin slices

Whisk balsamic vinegar, 3 teaspoons olive oil and thyme in a small bowl, pour over baby bocconcini and toss to combine. Wrap each cheese in a piece of prosciutto and set aside.

Brush bread slices with a little olive oil, place on an oven tray and bake at 180C for 5 minutes or until beginning to brown. Turn bread over, top each slice with proscuitto-wrapped bocconcini and drizzle with any remaining oil mixture. Bake for another 5-10 minutes or until bocconcini just begins to melt. Serve immediately.

wine: Pol Roger Brut Rosé, Epernay, France. Pink champagne is often dismissed as a frivolous and fun drink of little consequence. It's actually a rich and flavoursome Champagne style with a backbone of pinot noir and a splash of red wine to give it colour. That's not to say you can't enjoy it with these delicious croûtons.

time planner

one day ahead

● bake almond fingers: keep in airtight container

● cook crème anglaise: keep covered in refrigerator

on the day

● prepare dressing and vegetables for witlof salad

● prepare puddings and bake

● prepare beef, colcannon and vegetables, then cook

● wrap cheese in prosciutto, bake with croûtons and serve

● sear scallops and serve with salad

● rest beef, make sauce, then serve with colcannon and vegetables

● reheat crème anglaise and serve with warm puddings, followed by almond fingers

Luxury ingredients and
a succession of elegant
courses make a dinner that
says this is an occasion.
Match it with worthy wines
for an evening to remember.

SEARED SCALLOPS WITH WITLOF,
GINGER AND SESAME SALAD

SEARED SCALLOPS WITH WITLOF, GINGER AND SESAME SALAD

40 large scallops, roe removed
1 tablespoon peanut oil
1 teaspoon sesame oil

WITLOF, GINGER AND SESAME SALAD

2 teaspoons sesame seeds
1 teaspoon black sesame seeds
1 tablespoon peanut oil
2 teaspoons sesame oil
2 tablespoons lime juice
1 teaspoon finely grated ginger
1 teaspoon palm sugar
  or light brown sugar
1 tablespoon fish sauce
3 green onions, cut into 5cm lengths
  and julienned
1 large witlof, julienned
1 large red witlof, julienned

For witlof, ginger and sesame salad, roast sesame seeds in a frying pan over medium heat, stirring frequently until golden. Cool. Combine oils, lime juice, ginger, sugar and fish sauce, season to taste and whisk well.

Combine green onion and both witlof in a bowl of iced water with ice cubes and stand for 10 minutes, then drain and dry well in a clean tea towel.

Heat a heavy-based frying pan over high heat. Brush scallops with combined oils and cook over high heat for 30-60 seconds on each side or until golden and opaque.

Toss witlof and green onion with half the dressing and place in the middle of 8 plates. Place scallops around and drizzle with remaining dressing.

wine: Peter Lehmann Riesling, Eden Valley, SA. The sweet seafood flavours, the spiciness of the ginger and the nuttiness of the sesame seeds in this salad call for the fresh, crisp and citrus fruit flavours of riesling. This is a terrific example of the variety and a real bargain.

ROASTED FILLET OF BEEF WITH RED-WINE SAUCE

1 x 1.6kg eye fillet of beef, trimmed
2 teaspoons seeded mustard
1 tablespoon dijon mustard
2 teaspoons chopped oregano
1 tablespoon soft butter
1 cup rich veal stock (see basic recipes)
250ml dry red wine

Using kitchen string, tie fillet at 2cm intervals to form a neat shape. Combine mustards, oregano and butter, season to taste and rub all over fillet. Place beef in a lightly oiled roasting pan and roast at 180C for 1 hour for medium-rare or until cooked to your liking. Remove beef from pan and rest in a warm place for 10 minutes.

Meanwhile, skim fat from pan juices, then place pan over high heat and simmer for 1 minute. Add stock and simmer until reduced by half, then add wine and simmer until reduced by half, season to taste and strain through a fine sieve. Slice beef into 5mm-thick slices and serve with red-wine sauce, buttered steamed vegetables and colcannon (recipes follow).

wine: Grant Burge The Holy Trinity, Barossa Valley, SA. The trinity is of shiraz, grenache and mourvèdre grapes, the backbone of the great wines of France's Châteauneuf-du-Pape region. Grant Burge has blessed these varieties with good winemaking and some decent French oak. It is gutsy enough to stand up to the beef and the mustard – and a few years in the bottle.

BUTTERED STEAMED VEGETABLES

1 bunch of dutch carrots,
  peeled and tops trimmed
4 zucchini, cut into batons
200g snowpeas, topped
50g butter, chopped
1 shallot, chopped
2 tablespoons chopped mixed herbs,
  including thyme, oregano and
  flat-leaf parsley

Place carrots in a large bamboo steamer, cover and place over a wok of boiling water and steam for 5 minutes. Place zucchini and snowpeas on top of carrots and steam for another 5-10 minutes or until vegetables are tender.

Meanwhile, heat butter in a small saucepan, add shallot and cook over low heat for 4 minutes or until soft. Stir in herbs and pour over vegetables, season to taste and toss to combine.

ROASTED FILLET OF BEEF WITH RED-WINE SAUCE, COLCANNON AND BUTTERED STEAMED VEGETABLES

COLCANNON

1.25kg desirée potatoes,
  washed and dried
100g butter, chopped
1/2 cup pouring cream
1/2 cup milk
280g (2 cups) chopped savoy cabbage,
  blanched in boiling water
  for 1 minute, then drained
4 green onions, chopped
2 small shallots, chopped
6 slices pancetta, grilled until crisp,
  then broken into pieces
2 teaspoons chopped flat-leaf parsley

Place potatoes in a roasting pan and roast at 180C for 1-1 1/2 hours or until tender. Remove from oven and peel or scoop out flesh and push through a mouli or mash well with a potato masher. Combine butter, cream and milk in a saucepan and bring just to the boil, then gradually stir into mash. Stir in remaining ingredients, season to taste and mix well.

CHOCOLATE AND HAZELNUT PUDDING
WITH CREME ANGLAISE

CHOCOLATE AND HAZELNUT PUDDINGS WITH CREME ANGLAISE

200g dark couverture chocolate
  (70% cocoa solids), chopped
200g unsalted butter, chopped
4 eggs
3 egg yolks
110g ($^{1}/_{2}$ cup) caster sugar
110g ($^{3}/_{4}$ cup) plain flour
135g ($^{3}/_{4}$ cup) ground roasted hazelnuts
1$^{1}/_{4}$ cups crème anglaise
  (see basic recipes)

Melt chocolate and butter in the top of a double saucepan or in a heatproof bowl over simmering water, stirring occasionally, until glossy. Remove from heat.

Using an electric mixer, beat eggs, egg yolks and sugar until thick and pale, fold in sifted flour and ground hazelnuts, then stir in chocolate mixture and mix gently. Pour mixture into eight 200ml greased dariole moulds, place on a baking tray and bake at 180C for 25-30 minutes or until cooked when tested with a skewer. Carefully run a knife around edge of moulds, turn out and place warm puddings on 8 plates. Drizzle with warm crème anglaise.

wine: Campbells Wines Liqueur Gold Tokay, Rutherglen, Vic. Tokay is a unique Australian fortified wine made from muscadelle grapes which have been gently aged in old oak barrels. Cold tea, toffee and molasses are the classic flavour descriptors for tokay, and this wine shows them all.

ALMOND FINGERS

90g soft butter, chopped
55g ($^{1}/_{3}$ cup) icing sugar
1 tablespoon honey
1 egg yolk
150g (1 cup) plain flour
$^{1}/_{4}$ teaspoon baking powder
60g ($^{1}/_{2}$ cup) ground almonds

TOPPING

125g butter, chopped
2 tablespoons caster sugar
$^{1}/_{4}$ cup honey
100g (1$^{1}/_{4}$ cups) flaked almonds
100g ($^{2}/_{3}$ cup) macadamias, chopped

Beat butter, icing sugar and honey until light and fluffy, add egg yolk and beat until well combined. Stir in remaining ingredients and mix until a soft dough forms. Press mixture into a base-lined 20x30cm lamington pan and bake at 180C for 10-12 minutes or until lightly browned. Cool to room temperature.

For topping, combine butter, sugar and honey in a small saucepan and stir over low heat until butter melts and sugar dissolves. Increase heat and simmer for 3-5 minutes or until just golden, then stir in almonds and macadamias.

Pour topping over cooled base and bake at 180C for 10-15 minutes or until browned. Cool in pan, then cut into fingers.

ALMOND FINGERS

italian dinner party

time planner

in advance

● chicken stock can be made 3 days ahead:

keep covered in refrigerator

● pinenut biscuits can be made 3 days ahead:

keep in airtight container

one day ahead: keep covered in refrigerator

● cook veal and tomato ragù

● prepare polenta

on the day

● cook beans and vegetables for soup

● reheat veal and tomato ragù

● bake polenta and onions

● prepare salad and dressing

● add farro and scampi to soup and serve

● serve polenta with ragù and onions, toss salad

● whisk zabaglione and serve with strawberries

and pinenut biscuits

FARRO, CANNELLINI AND SCAMPI SOUP

Instead of farro puls polenta, you can use barley or short-grain white rice. Add 65g (¹/₃ cup) of either with the drained beans.

2 litres chicken stock (see basic recipes)
200g (1 cup) dried cannellini beans,
    soaked in cold water for 6 hours
    or overnight
2 zucchini, chopped
1 x 400g can crushed tomatoes
1 clove of garlic, chopped
2 small sprigs of rosemary
60g (¹/₃ cup) farro puls polenta
16 uncooked shelled scampi tails
8 small sage leaves,
    fried in 2 tablespoons
    hot olive oil, then drained
¹/₃ cup extra virgin olive oil

Bring stock to the boil in a large saucepan, add drained beans and simmer, covered, over low heat for 25 minutes. Add zucchini, tomato, garlic and rosemary sprigs and simmer, covered, for 20 minutes. Season to taste.

Sprinkle farro over soup and stir gently for 2 minutes. Remove rosemary sprigs. Add scampi and simmer for 2 minutes or until scampi just changes colour.

Serve soup in warm bowls, topped with a fried sage leaf and drizzled with a little extra virgin olive oil.

wine: Bollini Pinot Grigio, Trentino-Friuli, Italy. Pinot grigio (or pinot gris, as it is known in France's Alsace region) is a classic of the Trentino in north-eastern Italy. It has spicy, savoury characteristics with an underlying flavour of wild herbs. The finish is of zesty acidity which acts as a perfect counterpoint to the sweetness of the scampi.

Don't let a winter go by without gathering
a few friends for a big dinner. This Italian menu
– a hearty soup with the luxury of scampi,
the handsome looks of rich polenta stacks and
the heavenly lightness of a winey zabaglione
– goes beyond the dishes everyone knows.

FARRO, CANNELLINI AND SCAMPI SOUP

POLENTA WITH VEAL AND TOMATO RAGU AND BAKED ONIONS

1 teaspoon salt
600g instant polenta
60g soft unsalted butter, chopped
2 tablespoons extra virgin olive oil
1 small onion, chopped
2 sticks of celery, chopped
1 carrot, chopped
2 cloves of garlic, chopped
1 teaspoon thyme leaves
1 tablespoon chopped flat-leaf parsley
750g minced veal
125ml dry red wine
2 x 400g cans whole peeled tomatoes,
    drained and chopped
1 fresh, small red chilli, optional,
    finely chopped
500g bocconcini, sliced
100g Parmigiano Reggiano, grated

BAKED ONIONS

8 spanish onions, peeled
1 tablespoon chopped flat-leaf parsley
1 fresh, small red chilli, chopped
60g soft unsalted butter, chopped

Bring 2.5 litres water to the boil in a large saucepan and add salt. Gradually whisk in polenta and stir over medium heat for 3 minutes or until thick and polenta comes away from side of pan. Add butter and stir until melted, then season to taste with cracked black pepper. Spread polenta over two 30x40cm wet oven trays to a thickness of 1cm. Cool.

Heat olive oil in a large saucepan, add vegetables, garlic and herbs and cook for 10 minutes or until onion is soft. Add veal and, using a wooden spoon, stir for 10 minutes. Add wine and stir over heat until nearly evaporated. Add chopped tomato and chilli, if using, and simmer, covered, for 30 minutes or until mixture is thick. Season to taste.

Cut polenta into sixteen 10cm squares. Place half the squares 5cm apart on two oven trays, top with half the veal mixture and half the bocconcini. Repeat layering once more with remaining polenta, veal mixture and bocconcini, then sprinkle with parmesan.

Bake at 200C for 30-40 minutes or until cheese melts and polenta is hot. Stand for 5 minutes before serving.

VIN SANTO ZABAGLIONE
WITH STRAWBERRIES
AND PINENUT BISCUITS

Meanwhile, for baked onions, cut a deep cross halfway into each onion towards the root end. Combine parsley, chilli and butter in a small bowl and mix well. Divide butter mixture among onions, pressing it into cuts. Place onions in a small roasting pan and bake at 200C for 30 minutes or until cooked.

Carefully lift polenta and veal ragù onto 8 plates. Serve with baked onions and rocket and fennel salad (recipe follows).

wine: Frescobaldi Castiglioni Chianti, Tuscany, Italy. It's no accident that Chianti and rich, tomato-based sauces work well together, as sangiovese (the grape of Chianti) is blessed with mild tannins and naturally high acidity. This makes for a perfect combination with the sweet–acid flavours of good tomatoes.

ROCKET AND FENNEL SALAD

250g baby rocket
4 bulbs of baby fennel,
    trimmed, cored and sliced
2 witlof or red witlof, trimmed
    and leaves separated
1 ripe pomegranate,
    peeled and seeded

DRESSING

1/3 cup extra virgin olive oil
1 tablespoon lemon juice
1 teaspoon dijon mustard

For dressing, whisk olive oil, lemon juice, mustard and a pinch of sugar in a small bowl until combined, then season to taste.

Just before serving, combine salad ingredients in a large bowl, add dressing and toss well.

VIN SANTO ZABAGLIONE WITH STRAWBERRIES AND PINENUT BISCUITS

500g strawberries, hulled and sliced
8 large egg yolks
165g (3/4 cup) caster sugar
160ml vin santo or another dessert wine

PINENUT BISCUITS

160g (1 cup) blanched whole almonds
165g (3/4 cup) caster sugar
1 large egg white, lightly beaten
Few drops of almond essence
100g (2/3 cup) pinenuts
40g (1/4 cup) icing sugar

For pinenut biscuits, combine almonds and sugar in a food processor and process until finely ground, then transfer to a bowl. Add egg white and almond essence and stir until combined and mixture forms a firm dough. Stand biscuit dough at room temperature for 10 minutes. Roll teaspoons of mixture into balls, then roll in pinenuts, pressing gently to coat. Place biscuits 5cm apart on baking-paper-lined oven trays, then sprinkle lightly with sifted icing sugar. Bake at 180C for 10-12 minutes or until cooked. Cool on a wire rack.

Divide strawberries among eight 225ml-capacity glasses. Whisk egg yolks, sugar and wine in a large bowl until well combined. Place bowl over a pan of simmering water, without allowing the base of the bowl to touch the water, and whisk over low heat for 5 minutes or until thick and glossy.

Ladle warm vin santo zabaglione over strawberries in prepared glasses and serve immediately with pinenut biscuits.

Makes about 30 biscuits.

wine: Tenuta di Capezzana Vin Santo, Tuscany, Italy. Vin santo is a unique Italian white wine made from air-dried grapes. It shows a deliberate oxidative character which helps to restrain both the intensity and the sweetness, leaving the palate dry. This is an Italian curio.

simple vegetarian lunch

menu serves 4

carrot soup with dill

mushroom and buckwheat risotto with coriander pesto

poached honey pears with ricotta

CARROT SOUP WITH DILL

1/2 cup firmly packed dill leaves
1 cup sour cream
30g butter
1 tablespoon vegetable oil
1 onion, chopped
2 sticks of celery, chopped
1kg carrots, peeled and chopped
1 teaspoon smoky paprika
1.25 litres vegetable or chicken stock
  (see basic recipes)
Bouquet garni of mint, dill and bay leaves
1/3 cup lemon juice, or to taste

Process dill and sour cream in a food processor until well combined. Cover and refrigerate until needed.

Heat butter with oil in a large saucepan, add onion and cook over medium heat for 5 minutes or until onion is soft. Add celery, carrot and paprika, stir to combine and cook for 1 minute. Stir in stock and bouquet garni, cover and bring to the boil, then reduce heat and simmer for 30 minutes or until vegetables are soft.

Discard bouquet garni and purée carrot mixture, in batches, in a food processor until smooth. Return soup to pan, season with sea salt, cracked black pepper and lemon juice to taste and stir until heated through. Ladle soup into warm bowls and top with a spoonful of dill cream. Using a knife, swirl cream through soup.

wine: Margan Verdelho, Hunter Valley, NSW.

MUSHROOM AND BUCKWHEAT RISOTTO WITH CORIANDER PESTO

1 litre vegetable or chicken stock
  (see basic recipes)
10g dried porcini mushrooms,
  rinsed in cold water
2 tablespoons olive oil
1 leek, white part only, chopped
2 cloves of garlic, chopped
400g portobello or swiss brown
  mushrooms, chopped
200g (1 cup) raw buckwheat
200g (1 cup) arborio rice
20g butter

CORIANDER PESTO

1 cup firmly packed coriander leaves
50g parmesan, grated
1 clove of garlic, chopped
50g roasted pinenuts
100ml olive oil

For coriander pesto, process coriander, parmesan, garlic and pinenuts until well combined. With motor running, gradually add oil in a thin stream until mixture is smooth, then season to taste.

Bring stock to the boil, add porcini mushrooms, remove from heat and stand for 15 minutes or until mushrooms are soft. Using a slotted spoon, remove mushrooms and chop, then return stock to heat and keep at a low simmer.

Heat oil in a saucepan, add leek and cook over low heat until soft. Add garlic and portobello or swiss brown mushroom and stir over medium heat until mushroom is soft. Add chopped porcini mushroom, buckwheat and rice and stir to combine. Add 1 cup simmering stock and stir over low heat until stock is absorbed. Add remaining simmering stock 1/2 cup at a time, allowing each addition to be absorbed before adding the next, until buckwheat and rice are al dente. With the last addition of stock, stir in butter, season to taste and stand, covered, for 5 minutes before serving in warm bowls topped with a generous spoonful of coriander pesto.

wine: Evans & Tate Gnangara Shiraz, Margaret River, WA.

POACHED HONEY PEARS WITH RICOTTA

310ml dry white wine
165g (3/4 cup) caster sugar
1 vanilla bean, split lengthwise
2 strips of orange peel
4 firm william pears, peeled,
  quartered and cored
200g low-fat ricotta, drained
1/3 cup vanilla-bean honey or honey

Combine wine, sugar, vanilla bean, orange peel and 1 cup water in a deep frying pan and stir over low heat until sugar dissolves. Add pear, bring to the boil, then cover and simmer over low heat for 10 minutes or until pear is soft. Remove from heat and cool pear in liquid, then, using a slotted spoon, remove pear. Process ricotta with 2 tablespoons poaching liquid in a food processor until smooth. Reserve 1/3 cup poaching liquid.

Heat honey in a non-stick heavy-based frying pan, add pear, cut side down, and cook over high heat, turning once, for 6-8 minutes or until caramelised. Remove pear. Carefully add reserved poaching liquid to caramel and stir over medium heat until smooth. Spoon ricotta cream into 4 bowls, top with pear and drizzle with caramel sauce.

wine: Mitchelton Blackwood Park Botrytis Riesling, Nagambie Lakes, Vic.

You can make the soup and poach the pears as far ahead as you like, leaving only the risotto to prepare at mealtime. It will take only a few minutes to reheat the pears and serve them warm.

casual bistro lunch

time planner

in advance: keep covered in refrigerator

● soak salt cod 2 days ahead

one day ahead: keep covered in refrigerator

● prepare salt-cod brandade

● roast duck and garlic, cook soup

● combine roasted garlic with crème fraîche

● bake rosemary and black-onion-seed wafers:
keep in airtight container

on the day

● poach pears, prepare and bake charlottes

● reheat soup, shave fennel

● serve wafers, followed by brandade

● cook mushrooms, add to shaved-fennel salad
and serve with soup and roasted-garlic crème fraîche

● serve charlottes with ice-cream

ROSEMARY AND BLACK-ONION-SEED WAFERS

85g cheddar, grated
60g parmesan, grated
110g (3/4 cup) plain flour
80g butter, chopped
1 teaspoon worcestershire sauce
2 teaspoons finely chopped rosemary
1 teaspoon black onion seeds

Process cheeses, flour, butter and sauce in a food processor for about 2 minutes or until mixture resembles coarse breadcrumbs. Add rosemary and black onion seeds and pulse until just combined. Form mixture into a 2cm-thick disc, wrap in plastic wrap and refrigerate for at least 1 hour.

Cut dough into 5 equal pieces, place 1 piece on a lightly floured surface (return other pieces to refrigerator until ready to use) and roll out until 1mm thick. Tear dough into 3x12cm strips, place 3cm apart on baking-paper-lined oven trays and bake at 200C for 6 minutes or until edges are golden. Stand on trays for 5 minutes, then, using a flat spatula, carefully transfer to a wire rack to cool. Repeat with remaining dough.

Makes about 40.

This is traditional French bistro food – robust, simple and great for casual dining. This menu also works well as a lunch or dinner to have ready when you come in with friends from an outing.

ROSEMARY AND BLACK-ONION-SEED WAFERS

SALT-COD BRANDADE

SALT-COD BRANDADE

600g boneless fillet of salt cod
1 onion, thickly sliced
2 bay leaves
1/3 cup olive oil
250g pontiac potatoes, peeled,
    boiled and mashed (to make
    about 1 1/4 cups mashed potato)
3 cloves of garlic
3/4 cup pouring cream
2-3 teaspoons lemon juice
Truffle oil or extra virgin olive oil, to serve
Italian-style bread, to serve

Place cod in a large bowl, cover with water and refrigerate, covered, for 2 days, changing the water twice a day. Drain.

Combine onion, bay leaves and 1.5 litres water in a large saucepan and bring to the boil. Reduce heat to a slow simmer, add drained cod and poach gently for 10 minutes. Taste a piece from the thickest part and if it is still very salty poach for another 5 minutes. Drain cod and cool, discarding onion and bay leaves. Heat oil in a large saucepan for 1-2 minutes over very low heat until just warm, add cod and, using a whisk, stir and pound vigorously until it is well shredded, then stir in mashed potato.

Crush garlic in a mortar with a pestle and gradually add cream, pounding to incorporate. Stir cream mixture into salt-cod mixture and add lemon juice and cracked black pepper to taste. Drizzle with truffle oil or extra virgin olive oil and serve with Italian-style bread.

wine: Château Bonnet Blanc, Bordeaux, France. It was the Bordelaise who first combined semillon grapes with sauvignon blanc, producing a wine with delightful upfront herbal fruit flavours yet the structure and intensity to age for many years. The powerful, salty flavours of the brandade require a boldly flavoured white – the Château Bonnet will meet the challenge nicely.

DUCK AND LENTIL SOUP

DUCK AND LENTIL SOUP

1 x 1.5kg duck with giblets and neck
1 bulb of garlic (with at least 8 cloves)
1 tablespoon sherry vinegar
1 cup crème fraîche
3 litres chicken stock (see basic recipes)
1 tablespoon olive oil
200g pancetta, finely chopped
1 large spanish onion, finely chopped
2 carrots, chopped
3 sticks of celery, chopped
2 teaspoons mustard seeds
3 parsnips, chopped
350g Puy lentils, rinsed
2 granny smith apples, finely chopped

Rinse duck inside and out and pat dry with absorbent paper. Using a small, sharp knife, prick skin all over, then season inside and out with salt and cracked black pepper. Place duck, breast side down, on a wire rack in a roasting pan and roast at 200C for 30 minutes. Turn duck over and roast for another hour. Reduce heat to 150C, place garlic bulb and sherry vinegar in a small ovenproof dish and place in oven with duck, then roast for another 30-40 minutes or until juices run clear when thickest part of thigh is pierced with a skewer and garlic is tender. Rest duck for 20 minutes.

When garlic is cool enough to handle, squeeze into a bowl, add crème fraîche

and mix well. When duck is cool enough to handle, remove meat with skin from bones and cut into bite-sized pieces. Combine bones, stock, giblets and neck in a large saucepan, bring to the boil and simmer for 35 minutes to create a rich duck stock. Strain and discard solids.

Heat oil in a large saucepan, add pancetta, onion, carrot and celery and cook over medium heat for 5-7 minutes or until vegetables just begin to soften. Add mustard seeds and parsnip and cook for another 2 minutes. Add strained stock and bring to a simmer.

Meanwhile, cook lentils in boiling, salted water for 15 minutes or until almost cooked. Drain, add to soup mixture and cook for another 10 minutes until lentils are just tender. Season to taste, add apple and duck meat and cook for another 5 minutes until apple is just cooked but still slightly crunchy. Serve in warm bowls, topped with a dollop of roasted-garlic crème fraîche.

wine: Joseph Drouhin Côte de Nuits Villages, Burgundy, France. Duck and pinot noir is one of the classic wine and food marriages. While this pinot sits on the lower rungs of Burgundian hierarchy, it has full dark-cherry and earthy flavours with sufficient weight and body to combine well with the nutty flavours of the lentils in this gutsy soup.

SHAVED-FENNEL SALAD WITH WARM MUSHROOMS

Using a mandolin if possible, thinly shave fennel and place in a large bowl.

Heat 1-2 tablespoons oil in a large frying pan, add mushroom and cook over medium heat, stirring occasionally, for 2 minutes. Remove from heat and stir in herbs, lemon juice, spices and sea salt to taste. Add mushroom mixture to fennel and stir in remaining oil. Season to taste with extra oil and lemon juice if necessary and serve warm, sprinkled with parmesan.

CARAMELISED PEAR CHARLOTTES

100g (1/2 cup, firmly packed) brown sugar
125g unsalted butter, chopped
6 medium pears, peeled, cored
    and quartered, each quarter sliced
    lengthwise into 3
24 white bread slices, crusts removed
    and bread rolled gently
    with a rolling pin to flatten slightly
40g unsalted butter, extra, melted
Vanilla and raspberry swirl
    or vanilla ice-cream, to serve

Heat sugar and butter in a large frying pan over low heat until butter and sugar are melted and mixture is combined, if necessary adding 1-2 tablespoons boiling water to dissolve the sugar. Add pear and cook for 7-10 minutes or until just tender.

Cut 8 bread slices into rounds to fit the bases of eight 200ml-capacity dariole moulds, then cut each of remaining 16 slices into three 3x8cm strips. Brush both sides of rounds and strips with extra melted butter. Place rounds in the bases of moulds and line the sides with bread strips, overlapping the edges of bread and allowing the strips to overhang the tops. Using a slotted spoon, place 9 pear slices in each mould and fold overhanging bread over the top to create little closed peaks. Place on an oven tray and cover loosely with foil. Bake for 30 minutes until slightly golden, remove foil and bake for another 10 minutes or until golden and crisp on top. Serve caramelised pear charlottes warm in the moulds topped with a little ice-cream, or turn out and serve with ice-cream.

wine: Château Coutet à Barsac, Sauternes, France. Barsac is a subregion of Sauternes, and the wines of Château Coutet are the most highly regarded of the area. This one has flavours of ripe pears, nectarines and apricots. It also has a tight acid structure and subtle botrytis cinerea characters that don't overwhelm its prime fruit flavours.

SHAVED-FENNEL SALAD WITH WARM MUSHROOMS

2-3 bulbs of fennel
1/4 cup extra virgin olive oil
500g mixed mushrooms, including
    button, swiss brown and shiitake,
    sliced if large
1 tablespoon chopped chives
2 teaspoons chopped flat-leaf parsley
2 tablespoons lemon juice
1/2 teaspoon crushed coriander seeds
1/2 teaspoon crushed white peppercorns
Olive oil and lemon juice, extra, to taste
90g parmesan, grated

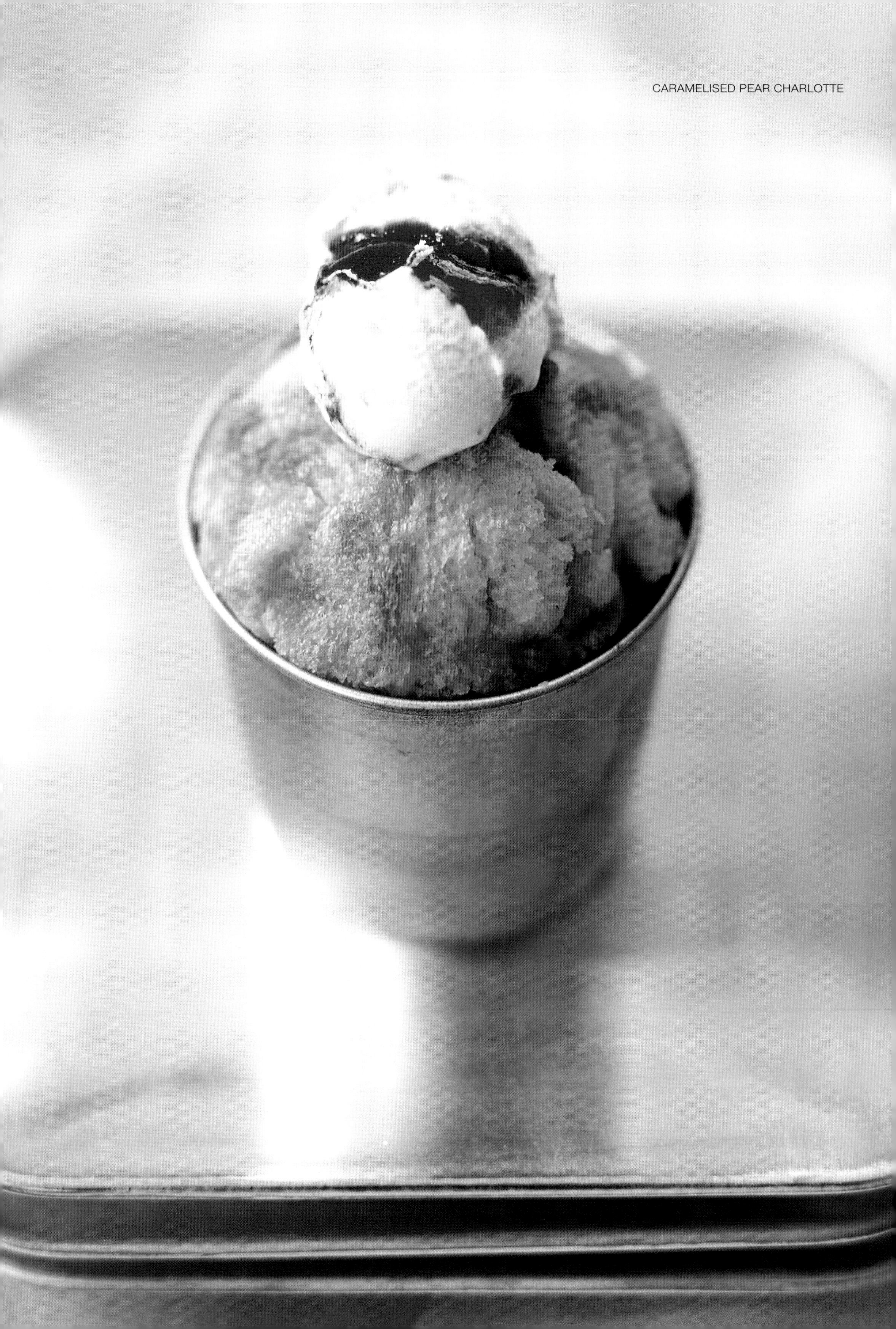

cosy sunday lunch

menu serves 8

roasted cumin-seed and orange olives

smoked-trout and fennel toasts with baby cos hearts and parsley dressing

lamb shanks with white beans and picada

glazed vanilla quince and rhubarb with chocolate pots

SMOKED-TROUT AND FENNEL TOASTS WITH
BABY COS HEARTS AND PARSLEY DRESSING

time planner

in advance: keep covered in refrigerator

• roasted cumin-seed and orange olives can be made,
without parsley, 1 week ahead

one day ahead: keep covered in refrigerator

• bake chocolate pots

• poach quince and rhubarb

• slow-roast lamb shanks with white beans

on the day

• prepare parsley dressing and fennel purée, toast bread

• make picada

• prepare trout and lettuce

• remove dessert from refrigerator

• add parsley to olives and serve

• serve trout with fennel toasts, lettuce and dressing

• reheat lamb shanks and serve with white beans and picada

• serve dessert

ROASTED CUMIN-SEED AND ORANGE OLIVES

2 teaspoons cumin seeds
2 teaspoons fennel seeds
2 cloves of garlic, very thinly sliced
5 x 5cm strips of orange rind
200g green olives stuffed
    with feta and semi-dried tomato,
    or other stuffed green olives
200g kalamata olives
200g small black olives
200g semi-dried tomatoes
1/4 cup olive oil
2 teaspoons balsamic vinegar
1/4 cup flat-leaf parsley leaves, torn

Combine seeds, garlic, orange rind, olives and semi-dried tomatoes in a small roasting pan, drizzle with oil, then toss well to combine. Roast at 200C, stirring occasionally, for 15-20 minutes or until olives begin to wrinkle slightly. Remove from oven, add balsamic vinegar and parsley, season to taste with freshly ground black pepper and mix well.

Serve olives warm or at room temperature. Makes about 5 cups.

wine: Mildara Supreme Dry Sherry, Riverland, SA. As the marketplace continues to move towards table wines, this classic dry sherry – the perfect aperitif – has almost been lost. Sherry and olives is a traditional Spanish pairing, the sherry having sufficient weight and flavour to counterpoint the intense flavours in the roasted olives.

A marvellous meal for a cold night,
or for one of those leisurely, casual
winter lunches that go on all afternoon.

SMOKED-TROUT AND FENNEL TOASTS WITH BABY COS HEARTS AND PARSLEY DRESSING

8 slices of Italian-style bread,
    brushed with olive oil and grilled
    until golden and crisp
1 smoked trout (about 200g),
    skin and bones removed and flesh
    flaked into about 16 large chunks
4 baby cos lettuces, outer leaves
    removed, quartered lengthwise

PARSLEY DRESSING

1 cup firmly packed
    flat-leaf parsley leaves
1/2 cup olive oil
1/4 cup verjuice

FENNEL PUREE

30g unsalted butter, chopped
3 bulbs of baby fennel (about 635g),
    cored, trimmed and thinly sliced
1 small desirée potato (120g),
    peeled and coarsely grated
1 tablespoon verjuice
    or 2 teaspoons lemon juice

For parsley dressing, place parsley in a bowl, cover with boiling water, then drain and refresh immediately in ice-cold water. Drain parsley and squeeze out excess moisture. Process parsley and 1/4 teaspoon salt in a food processor until finely chopped, then, with the motor running, add oil in a slow, steady stream until combined. Add verjuice and process until just combined. Strain dressing through a fine sieve, then season to taste with cracked black pepper.

For fennel purée, melt butter in a small frying pan, add fennel and potato and cook, covered, stirring occasionally, over medium heat for 20 minutes or until vegetables are very tender. Process fennel mixture and verjuice or lemon juice in a food processor until smooth, then push mixture through a fine sieve and season to taste.

Spread toasted bread slices with warm fennel purée, top each with 2 pieces of smoked trout. Place on 8 plates with cos wedges drizzled with parsley dressing to one side.

wine: Crawford River Semillon Sauvignon Blanc, Henty, Vic. The smokiness of the trout and the subtle herbal aniseed flavours of the fennel require a flavoursome white which is not big, bold or overpowering. This Crawford River white is fresh, vital and full-flavoured.

LAMB SHANKS WITH WHITE BEANS AND PICADA

8 lamb shanks
    (about 220g each), frenched
2 tablespoons olive oil
2 onions, finely chopped
1 large carrot, finely chopped
250ml dry red wine
2 red capsicum, roasted and peeled
    (see basic recipes) and cut into
    4cm-wide strips
1.25 litres veal or chicken stock
    (see basic recipes)
2 x 400g cans whole peeled
    tomatoes, chopped
300g (1 1/2 cups) dried white beans,
    soaked overnight in cold water

PICADA

2 tablespoons olive oil
2 thick slices of Italian-style
    bread, quartered
6 cloves of garlic, flattened
1 tablespoon rosemary leaves
55g (1/3 cup) blanched almonds, roasted
1/2 tablespoon flat-leaf parsley, chopped

Heat a large, heavy-based casserole, add shanks, in batches, and cook over medium-high heat until browned all over (shanks will oil the pan), then drain on absorbent paper. Discard oil in pan and heat olive oil. Add onion and carrot and cook over low heat for 5 minutes, then add wine and bring to the boil. Simmer wine mixture until reduced by half, add capsicum, stock and chopped tomatoes and their juice and bring to the boil.

Place drained beans and shanks in a single layer in a large roasting pan, pour sauce mixture over, cover tightly with foil and cook at 160C for 1 1/2-1 3/4 hours or until meat is very tender and beginning to fall off the bone.

Meanwhile, for picada, heat oil in a frying pan, add bread and fry quickly over medium heat until golden, then drain on absorbent paper. Add garlic and rosemary to pan and stir over heat for 2 minutes or until garlic is golden. Process bread, garlic mixture and blanched almonds in a food processor until coarsely chopped. Transfer to a small bowl and add parsley.

Strain cooking liquid from shank and bean mixture into a saucepan, reduce oven temperature to 100C, cover shanks and beans and return to oven to keep warm. Simmer strained cooking juices over high heat until reduced by half and of a syrupy consistency. Add half the picada and mix well, then add to lamb shanks and stir through to combine.

Place lamb shanks, white beans and sauce in 8 large, warm bowls and serve sprinkled with remaining picada.

wine: Bannockburn Shiraz, Geelong, Vic. Gary Farr, Bannockburn's dedicated winemaker, produces one of the best European styles of shiraz in the country. Intense savoury flavours abound in this complex and earthy shiraz – it's perfect for this gutsy dish.

GLAZED VANILLA QUINCE AND RHUBARB WITH CHOCOLATE POTS

3 cups milk
1 cup pouring cream
1 tablespoon strong espresso coffee
    or 1 teaspoon instant espresso
    coffee granules
200g dark bittersweet Belgian
    chocolate (60-70% cocoa solids),
    finely chopped
10 egg yolks
100g (1/2 cup, firmly packed)
    brown sugar

GLAZED VANILLA QUINCE AND RHUBARB

310g trimmed rhubarb
    (about 1 bunch), chopped
220g (1 cup) caster sugar
2 vanilla beans, split lengthwise
125ml ruby port
Zested rind and juice of 1 lemon
4 quince (about 1.5kg), peeled,
    cored and each cut into 8 wedges

For glazed vanilla quince and rhubarb, combine rhubarb, sugar, vanilla beans, port, lemon rind and juice and 3½ cups water in a large, heavy-based saucepan and stir over low-medium heat until sugar dissolves. Bring to a simmer and cook for 3-5 minutes or until rhubarb is just tender. Using a slotted spoon, remove rhubarb, place in a large bowl, cool, cover and refrigerate until needed. Add quince to pan and cook, covered, for 30 minutes, then uncover and cook for another hour or until quince is rust-coloured, tender and cooking liquid is thick and syrupy. Cool. (Do not stir, as quince will be delicate – it will firm on cooling.) Add quince mixture to rhubarb in bowl and mix gently to combine.

Combine milk, cream and coffee in a small saucepan and bring to a gentle simmer, stirring granules, if using, until dissolved. Remove from heat immediately, add chocolate and stir until smooth and chocolate has melted. Beat egg yolks and sugar in a bowl with an electric mixer until well combined. Gradually add chocolate mixture to egg mixture and mix to combine. Divide chocolate mixture among eight 150ml-capacity pots or ramekins. Line a baking pan with baking paper, then place pots in pan and add enough boiling water to come halfway up side of dishes. Bake at 180C for 20-25 minutes or until just set. Refrigerate for 5 hours or overnight until firm.

Serve small glasses of glazed vanilla quince and rhubarb with chocolate pots.
wine: Yalumba Museum Release Old Liqueur Muscat, Barossa Valley, SA. Chocolate is the kiss of death to traditional dessert wines. It needs a big, bold and syrupy muscat with strong fruit flavours and a high alcohol content. This delicious muscat from Yalumba is robust enough to match both the chocolate and the intense flavours of the quince.

simple asian lunch

PEPPERED SESAME PRAWNS AND CALAMARI ON CUCUMBER SALAD

2 teaspoons cracked black pepper
2 teaspoons sesame seeds
2 teaspoons sea salt
2 tablespoons plain flour
1 large calamari (about 300g),
    cleaned and skinned
12 uncooked prawns, peeled
    and deveined, leaving tails intact
2 teaspoons sesame oil
1/4 cup peanut oil

CUCUMBER SALAD

2 sticks of celery, sliced on the diagonal
1 lebanese cucumber,
    sliced on the diagonal
1 baby bok choy, washed
    and thinly sliced
1 1/2 tablespoons light soy sauce
3 teaspoons rice vinegar
1/4 teaspoon chilli oil

For cucumber salad, combine celery, cucumber and baby bok choy in a bowl. Combine soy sauce, vinegar and chilli oil, whisk well, pour over salad and toss to combine.

Combine pepper, sesame seeds, salt and flour in a bowl and mix well. Using a small, sharp knife, score inside of calamari, then cut into 2x6cm pieces. Toss calamari and prawns in flour mixture, in batches, and shake away excess. Heat sesame and peanut oil in a wok until just smoking and stir-fry calamari and prawns, in batches, over high heat for 2-3 minutes or until golden, then drain on absorbent paper. Serve seafood on a bed of cucumber salad.

wine: Rosemount Estate Semillon Sauvignon Blanc, Hunter Valley, NSW.

TAMARIND CHICKEN WITH EGGPLANT

Peanut oil
5 japanese eggplant (about 325g),
    sliced on the diagonal
600g chicken thigh fillets,
    cut into 3cm pieces
1 onion, cut into thin wedges
2 tablespoons grated ginger
3 kaffir-lime leaves, thinly sliced
1 tablespoon finely chopped lemongrass
1 fresh, small red chilli, finely chopped
2 tablespoons lime juice
1 teaspoon caster sugar
2 tablespoons fish sauce
2 1/2 tablespoons tamarind paste
1/3 cup coriander leaves
    and steamed rice, to serve

Heat 2 tablespoons peanut oil in a wok and stir-fry eggplant, in batches, over high heat until golden. Remove from wok. Add a little extra oil and stir-fry chicken, in batches, over high heat until golden. Remove from wok. Add onion and ginger and cook over high heat for 3-4 minutes. Add remaining ingredients, chicken and eggplant and simmer for 5-10 minutes until chicken is tender. Stir in coriander leaves and serve with steamed rice.

wine: Tatachilla Chardonnay, McLaren Vale, SA.

APPLE AND GINGER BRIOCHE PUDDING

50g butter, chopped
2 granny smith apples,
    peeled, cored and sliced
25g drained ginger in syrup, thinly sliced
1 tablespoon maple syrup
6 x 1.5cm-thick slices of brioche
    (about 175g)
3/4 cup milk
1/2 cup pouring cream
55g (1/4 cup) caster sugar
2 eggs
1/2 teaspoon ground cinnamon
1/4 teaspoon ground nutmeg
1 tablespoon warmed redcurrant
    or quince jelly, to glaze
Vanilla ice-cream, to serve

Melt butter in a frying pan, add apple, ginger and maple syrup and cook over medium-high heat for 5 minutes or until apple is tender. Remove from heat.

Stand brioche slices upright in a buttered 4-cup-capacity ovenproof dish. Place apple mixture between brioche slices and drizzle with apple juices.

Whisk milk, cream, sugar, eggs and spices in a bowl, then slowly pour over brioche, allowing the mixture to soak in. Place dish in a large roasting pan and pour in enough boiling water to come halfway up side. Bake at 160C for 50 minutes until set. Brush with glaze and serve with ice-cream.

wine: Margan Botrytis Semillon, Hunter Valley, NSW.

An indulgent pudding calls for the rest of the
meal to be fresh-tasting and not too heavy.
Two quick-to-prepare courses – seafood
and salad, then chicken – fit the bill nicely.

warming winter lunch

time planner

one day ahead: keep covered in refrigerator

- make winter fruit salad
- make buttermilk pudding

on the day

- roast tomatoes, crumb eggplant
- prepare garlic and chilli paste, rub over pork and roast with shallots
- cook pea mixture
- deep-fry eggplant and serve with tomato and basil
- place polenta on to cook
- remove winter fruit salad from refrigerator
- cook pasta and serve with pea mixture
- serve pork with shallots and polenta
- serve winter fruit salad with pudding

CRUMBED EGGPLANT WITH ROASTED TOMATOES AND BASIL

12 cherry tomatoes, halved
1 tablespoon olive oil
2-3 japanese eggplant
    (depending on size)
75g (1/2 cup) plain flour,
    seasoned with salt and pepper
2 eggs, lightly beaten
75g (1 cup) panko
Vegetable oil, for shallow-frying
24 small basil leaves

Toss tomato in oil, place on a lightly greased oven tray, season with sea salt and cracked black pepper and roast at 150C for 45 minutes or until semi-dried.

Cut eggplant into about 24 slices 5mm thick, dust with seasoned flour and shake away excess. Dip each slice in beaten egg, then in panko. Shallow-fry eggplant, in batches, in hot vegetable oil until golden on both sides. Drain on absorbent paper.

Place half a roasted cherry tomato and a basil leaf on each piece of eggplant and serve immediately.

wine: Clover Hill Sparkling Brut, Piper's River, Tas. Tasmania is emerging as one of the best producers of premium sparkling wine. Made by Taltarni, this Clover Hill has fine, delicate fruit flavours that complement the sweetness of the tomatoes and the spiciness of the basil. The fresh, crisp, appley acid finish helps to cut through the richness of the crumbed eggplant.

Comforting, sustaining ... all the good words fit.
This menu is full of ideas for other meals, too – the
pork for a make-at-the-weekend, eat-on-a-weeknight
dinner, the spaghetti for a relaxed family meal, the
fruit salad to have with ice-cream, and the eggplant
as an accompaniment to a roast or grill.

SPAGHETTI WITH PEAS AND CHICORY

1/4 cup olive oil
1 onion, thinly sliced
1kg peas, podded to give
    400g (2 1/4 cups)
2 1/2 cups chicken stock
    (see basic recipes) or water
1 tablespoon shredded basil
2 cups coarsely chopped chicory
    or curly endive leaves
500g dried spaghetti, broken in half
Extra virgin olive oil and
    coarsely grated provolone, to serve

Heat oil in a saucepan and cook onion over low heat until soft. Add peas and stock or water, bring to the boil, then simmer over very low heat for about 1 hour or until peas are very tender, adding a little more stock or water if they begin to stick to pan. Add basil and chicory or endive and cook over low heat until chicory or endive is just wilted.

Cook spaghetti in boiling, salted water until al dente, then drain and toss with a little extra virgin olive oil.

Place pasta in warm bowls, spoon pea mixture over, drizzle with extra virgin olive oil and sprinkle with provolone.

wine: Cockfighter's Ghost Semillon, Broke, NSW. This wine's pristine semillon fruit flavours of citrus, fresh herbs and lanolin are refreshed by the crisp lemony acidity. They will combine well with the sweetness of the peas and the savoury flavour of the chicory.

BRAISED PORK NECK WITH GARLIC AND CHILLI PASTE

6 cloves of garlic, crushed
2 fresh, small red chillies,
    finely chopped
1 teaspoon fennel seeds
2 teaspoons chopped thyme
1 x 1kg pork neck
Olive oil
12 shallots, peeled
2 cups chicken stock (see basic recipes)
2 tablespoons white-wine vinegar
1 teaspoon honey
250ml dry white wine
Soft polenta (see basic recipes), to serve

Pound garlic, chilli, fennel seeds, thyme and a pinch of salt in a mortar with a pestle until a paste forms. Using a small, sharp knife, make 10 incisions at equal distances over top of pork, then push a little paste mixture into each incision. Using kitchen string, tie pork at 2cm intervals, then rub any remaining paste over top. Heat 2 tablespoons oil in a large saucepan, add pork and shallots and cook over medium heat until pork is browned all over. Remove pork from pan, add stock and stir bottom of pan to pick up any sediment, then add vinegar, honey and wine and bring to the boil. Return pork to pan, reduce heat and simmer, covered, over low-medium heat for 45 minutes, then simmer, uncovered, for 20-30 minutes or until tender. Remove pork and shallots from pan, cover with foil and rest in a warm place for 10 minutes. Increase heat and boil sauce until reduced to 1 cup.

Spoon soft polenta onto warm plates, top with sliced pork and spoon shallots and sauce around.

wine: Mitchell The Growers Grenache, Clare Valley, SA. Grenache is a full-flavoured variety, especially when the vineyard yields are controlled. Here, the rich, gamy, dark plum and violet flavours are unencumbered by oak. The tannins are bold but neither hard nor bitter, so they avoid clashing with the spices in this dish.

WINTER FRUIT SALAD
WITH BUTTERMILK PUDDING

180g caster sugar
1/2 vanilla bean, split lengthwise
200ml pouring cream
8g (about 9 leaves) of gelatine,
    soaked in cold water for 5 minutes
600ml buttermilk

WINTER FRUIT SALAD
16 dried figs, hard tops removed
200g caster sugar
Juice and thinly sliced rind
    of 1 orange and 1/2 lemon
1 vanilla bean, split lengthwise
1 cinnamon stick
16 pitted prunes
16 dried apricots
16 dried peaches
2 oranges and lemons,
    extra, segmented

For winter fruit salad, cover figs with boiling water, stand for 1 hour, then drain. Combine sugar, citrus juices and 200ml water in a small saucepan and stir over medium heat until sugar dissolves. Add vanilla bean and cinnamon stick and cook gently for 10 minutes. Place citrus rind in a small saucepan, cover with water and bring to the boil. Drain and add rind to syrup with soaked figs and remaining dried fruit and poach for 30 minutes or until fruit is soft. Cool to room temperature, then add extra citrus segments.

Combine sugar, scraped seeds of vanilla bean (reserve bean for another use) and half the cream in a small saucepan and stir over low heat until sugar dissolves, then bring mixture just to the boil. Squeeze out water from gelatine, add gelatine to cream mixture and stir until gelatine dissolves. Cool mixture until tepid, then add buttermilk and mix well. Transfer to a bowl and place bowl in a larger bowl of ice and stir frequently until buttermilk mixture has cooled. As soon as mixture begins to thicken, beat remaining cream until soft peaks form, then add a quarter to buttermilk mixture and stir until smooth. Add remaining whipped cream and gently fold in until just combined. Cover and refrigerate for at least 3 hours or until set.

Serve spoonfuls of buttermilk pudding with winter fruit salad.

wine: Yalumba Noble Pick Botrytis Riesling, Eden Valley, SA. Riesling again shows its versatility, here as a dessert wine. Intense apricot and white-peach flavours are carefully overlaid with hints of rich caramel botrytis flavours which add character and complexity without overpowering the classic fruit flavours of this variety.

simple light dinner

MUSSELS WITH WHITE WINE AND GREMOLATA

120ml dry white wine
1/2 cup chicken stock (see basic recipes)
2 fresh, small red chillies,
    seeded and chopped
4 green onions, chopped
2kg black mussels,
    scrubbed and bearded
Italian-style bread, to serve

GREMOLATA

2 tablespoons chopped flat-leaf parsley
2 tablespoons chopped basil
2 cloves of garlic, finely chopped
1 tablespoon grated lemon rind

For gremolata, combine all ingredients and season to taste.

Combine wine, stock, chilli and green onion in a large stockpot and simmer over high heat until reduced by half. Add mussels, cover and cook over medium heat until mussels open (discard any that do not open). Transfer mussels to 4 warm bowls, season cooking liquid to taste and pour over. Sprinkle mussels with gremolata and serve immediately with Italian-style bread.
wine: Fermoy Estate Semillon, Margaret River, WA.

SEARED KANGAROO WITH BEETROOT AND BRAISED LEEKS

1/4 cup chicken stock (see basic recipes)
350g beetroot (about 2),
    peeled and grated
1 teaspoon thyme leaves
1 tablespoon balsamic vinegar
1 x 600g kangaroo rump
Olive oil
Wilted spinach, to serve

BRAISED LEEKS

2 teaspoons olive oil
4 leeks, white part only,
    halved lengthwise and crosswise
1/4 cup chicken stock (see basic recipes)

For braised leeks, heat oil in a saucepan, add leek and cook over medium heat for 1 minute. Add stock, season to taste, cover and cook over low heat for 10 minutes or until leek is tender.

Heat chicken stock in a saucepan, add beetroot, thyme and vinegar, season to taste and cook over medium heat until liquid is reduced and beetroot is just tender.

Rub kangaroo with a little oil and cracked black pepper. Brown all over in a hot non-stick frying pan over a high heat, transfer to a roasting pan and roast at 200C for 15-20 minutes. Remove from oven and rest in a warm place for 10 minutes.

Spoon wilted spinach onto 4 warm plates, top with leeks and sliced kangaroo and serve with beetroot.
wine: Geoff Merrill Shiraz, McLaren Vale, SA.

VANILLA SOUFFLES WITH CARAMELISED PINEAPPLE

2 cups chopped pineapple
2 tablespoons brown sugar
Icing sugar, to serve

VANILLA SOUFFLES

4 eggs, separated
1 tablespoon caster sugar
1 tablespoon plain flour
2 teaspoons vanilla extract

Combine pineapple and brown sugar in a non-stick frying pan and cook over high heat for 5 minutes or until pineapple is golden and slightly caramelised.

For vanilla soufflés, combine egg yolks, sugar, flour and vanilla extract and whisk until smooth. Whisk egg whites until soft peaks form, then gently fold into yolk mixture in 2 batches.

Spoon mixture into four 3/4-cup-capacity ramekins that have been lightly greased and sprinkled with sugar. Place ramekins on an oven tray and bake at 200C for 5-10 minutes or until soufflés have risen and are golden. Dust with icing sugar and serve immediately with little pots of caramelised pineapple.
wine: Brokenwood Jelka Vineyard Riesling, McLaren Vale, SA.

This dinner is big on flavour but low on fat.
Showcasing, as it does, our seafood, kangaroo
and tropical fruit, it's also a good one to bear
in mind if you have guests from overseas.

mediterranean dinner

time planner

one day ahead: keep covered in refrigerator

- cook tomato and rosemary sauce
- bake crème caramel

on the day

- prepare fennel and salad dressing and combine
- cook potatoes and prepare gnocchi
- cook prosciutto, assemble salad and serve
- cook gnocchi, sear tuna, reheat tomato sauce and serve
- serve crème caramel

CRISP PROSCIUTTO AND SHAVED-FENNEL SALAD

2 bulbs of fennel, trimmed,
  halved and cored
100g small black olives
1 tablespoon olive oil
200g thinly sliced prosciutto
100g pecorino, shaved
Extra virgin olive oil

DRESSING
Zested rind of 2 oranges
1/3 cup orange juice
1 tablespoon red-wine vinegar
1/4 teaspoon orange oil
2 tablespoons extra virgin olive oil
1 tablespoon coarsely chopped dill

Using a mandolin, thinly slice fennel and combine with olives.

For dressing, combine all ingredients, season to taste and whisk until well combined. Pour dressing over fennel mixture and toss to combine. Stand for 30 minutes for flavours to develop.

Heat olive oil in a non-stick frying pan and cook prosciutto, in batches, turning once, over medium heat until crisp. Spoon fennel salad onto 6 plates, top with crisp prosciutto and shaved pecorino, drizzle with extra virgin olive oil and sprinkle with cracked black pepper.

wine: Chain of Ponds Novello Rosé, Adelaide Hills, SA. The strong saltiness of the prosciutto and the intense aniseed flavour of fennel need a flavoursome wine with a touch of sweetness. This fresh, fruity rosé is just the trick – serve it well chilled.

When the main dish is one that will need some attention during the course of the meal, like the tuna, choose a dessert you can make ahead and an entrée that is little more than a matter of buying great ingredients and combining them attractively.

COFFEE AND VANILLA-BEAN CREME CARAMEL

COFFEE AND VANILLA-BEAN CRÈME CARAMEL

100g caster sugar
1/4 cup strong espresso coffee
2 eggs
3 egg yolks
75g (1/3 cup) caster sugar, extra
1 cup milk
1 1/3 cups pouring cream
2 teaspoons coffee beans,
  lightly crushed
1 vanilla bean, split lengthwise

Combine sugar and 1/4 cup water in a saucepan and stir over low heat until sugar dissolves. Increase heat and boil, without stirring, until mixture is golden. Remove from heat and carefully pour in coffee, return to heat and stir until smooth, then simmer for another 2 minutes. Pour caramel into six 1/2-cup-capacity ramekins.

Whisk eggs, egg yolks and extra sugar until combined. Combine milk, cream, coffee beans, scraped seeds of vanilla bean and bean in a saucepan and bring just to the boil. Remove from heat and stand for 10 minutes. Strain milk mixture into egg mixture, whisk to combine, then pour evenly among prepared ramekins.

Place ramekins in a large baking dish and pour in enough boiling water to come halfway up side of dishes. Bake at 180C for 30 minutes or until custard is just set.

Remove ramekins from baking dish, cool to room temperature, then cover and refrigerate for at least 6 hours or overnight.

Carefully run a knife around edge of ramekins and turn out crème caramels onto plates.

wine: Sevenhill Liqueur Frontignac, Clare Valley, SA. The frontignac grape is a more elegant member of the exuberant muscat family. It shows abundant intense dried-fruit flavours which have been tamed and concentrated by long maturation in old oak barrels.

PAN-FRIED TUNA WITH SPINACH GNOCCHI AND TOMATO AND ROSEMARY SAUCE

2 x 400g cans whole tomatoes
2 cloves of garlic, chopped
Olive oil
2 teaspoons rosemary leaves
2 fresh, small red chillies,
  seeded and chopped
6 tuna steaks (about 200g each)

SPINACH GNOCCHI
2 small bunches of spinach,
  trimmed and washed
750g pink-eye or desirée potatoes
75g (1/2 cup) plain flour, approximately
3 egg yolks
100g grated parmesan
3/4 teaspoon grated nutmeg

For spinach gnocchi, place spinach in a saucepan, cover with a lid and cook over medium heat until just wilted. Refresh under cold water, then squeeze out excess water and chop finely. You need 1/2 cup chopped spinach.

Place unpeeled potatoes in a saucepan with a little water and cover. Bring to the boil, simmer until cooked, then drain. When cool enough to handle, peel and mash potatoes, then stir in chopped spinach. Place potato mixture on a bench, make a well in the centre, add two-thirds of the flour, the egg yolks, a good pinch of salt, the parmesan and grated nutmeg. Using your hands, fold mixture continually towards the centre, adding a little more flour if necessary. Cover mixture with plastic wrap and rest for 5 minutes. Roll mixture into logs about 3cm in diameter, sprinkling with flour as you go, then cut logs into 3cm pieces.

Poach gnocchi in gently boiling, salted water until they rise to the surface. Drain.

Meanwhile, combine crushed tomatoes and their juice, garlic, a pinch of sugar, 2 tablespoons olive oil, rosemary and chilli and cook over medium heat until thick. Season to taste.

Heat a little olive oil in a large frying pan and cook tuna on both sides until just cooked. Place tuna and gnocchi in shallow bowls and spoon a little tomato sauce over.

wine: Mount Pleasant Elizabeth Semillon, Hunter Valley, NSW. Elizabeth Semillon is a Hunter Valley classic. Its dry toast and dried herbal flavours have both the weight and the complexity to combine well with the strong flavours of tuna, spinach and tomato. The bone-dry finish helps to cleanse the palate.

light asian dinner

** serves 6

prawn and water-chestnut dumplings with vinegar soy sauce

sang choi bau

roasted coral trout on hokkien noodles with shiitake mushrooms and broth

steamed asian greens with oyster sauce

mandarin jellies with melon

PRAWN AND WATER-CHESTNUT
DUMPLINGS WITH VINEGAR SOY SAUCE

time planner

one day ahead: keep covered in refrigerator

● prepare mandarin jellies

on the day

● marinate melon in verjuice syrup

● prepare dumplings and dipping sauce

● soak dried mushrooms

● steam dumplings and serve with dipping sauce

● prepare and serve sang choi bau

● roast trout, cook noodles, steam asian greens and serve

● serve mandarin jellies with melon

PRAWN AND WATER-CHESTNUT DUMPLINGS WITH VINEGAR SOY SAUCE

300g medium uncooked prawns,
    peeled, deveined and chopped
1/3 cup drained chopped water chestnuts
3 green onions, finely chopped
2 teaspoons finely chopped ginger
1 stem bok choy, leaves only,
    halved lengthwise and thinly sliced
1 teaspoon light soy sauce
2 teaspoons oyster sauce
2 teaspoons shaohsing rice wine
1 teaspoon cornflour
18 round egg-pastry wrappers
1 egg white, lightly beaten

VINEGAR SOY SAUCE

2 teaspoons dark soy sauce
2 teaspoons light soy sauce
3 teaspoons white vinegar
1/2 teaspoon chilli oil
1 green onion, white part only,
    finely chopped
1 1/2 tablespoons chicken stock
    (see basic recipes)

Combine prawn, water chestnut, green onion, ginger and bok choy in a bowl. Whisk sauces, rice wine and cornflour until combined, stir into prawn mixture and mix well.

Place 2 teaspoons of mixture in centre of each wrapper, brush edge with egg white and bring sides together to meet in the middle to form three points, then seal edge. Cover and refrigerate for up to 4 hours.

For vinegar soy sauce, combine all ingredients and stand for 1 hour before serving.

Place dumplings, in batches, in the top of a baking-paper-lined bamboo steamer, making sure dumplings do not touch each other. Brush edge of each dumpling with water, cover steamer, then place over a wok of boiling water and steam for about 10-15 minutes or until tender. Serve immediately with vinegar soy sauce.

Makes 18.

When you're looking for ways to eat lightly
but well, look to the Asian techniques
of steaming, of combining small quantities
of meat with vegetables and of serving
delicious noodle mixtures in broth.

ROASTED CORAL TROUT ON
HOKKIEN NOODLES WITH SHIITAKE
MUSHROOMS AND BROTH

SANG CHOI BAU

1 tablespoon vegetable oil
4 shallots, chopped
2 cloves of garlic, finely chopped
400g minced lean chicken
1/2 cup coarsely chopped
   water chestnuts
1/3 cup coarsely chopped
   fresh black fungus
1/4 cup shaohsing rice wine
1 tablespoon soy sauce
1 1/2 tablespoons oyster sauce
2 tablespoons chicken stock
   (see basic recipes) or water
2 green onions, thinly sliced
   on the diagonal
40g (1/2 cup) beansprouts
6 iceberg lettuce leaves, washed
   and trimmed to form a cup shape

Heat oil in a small frying pan, add shallot and garlic and cook over medium heat for 2 minutes. Add chicken and stir over heat for 2 minutes or until changed in colour, then stir in water chestnuts and fungus and cook for another 2 minutes. Add rice wine, sauces and stock or water, bring to the boil, then reduce heat and simmer for 4-5 minutes or until liquid is slightly reduced and thickened. Add green onion and beansprouts and cook for 1 minute. Spoon chicken mixture into lettuce cups and serve immediately.

wine: Nepenthe Riesling, Adelaide Hills, SA. Riesling is a very site-specific grape variety which has recently found a new home in the Adelaide Hills region. This riesling supports the claim that Nepenthe winemaker Peter Leske is one of Australia's most competent winemakers.

ROASTED CORAL TROUT ON HOKKIEN NOODLES WITH SHIITAKE MUSHROOMS AND BROTH

Peanut oil
6 coral trout fillets
   (about 200g each), skinned
500g fresh egg noodles
1 litre chicken or fish stock
   (see basic recipes)
1 tablespoon julienned ginger
1 small carrot, julienned
6 dried shiitake mushrooms,
   soaked in 1 cup boiling water
   for 10 minutes or until soft,
   then drained and sliced
4 green onions, julienned
1 1/2 tablespoons light soy sauce
1/3 cup shaohsing rice wine

Heat 1 tablespoon peanut oil in a heavy-based frying pan. Season coral trout with sea salt and cracked black pepper and cook fish, in batches, for 2-3 minutes on one side or until golden, then turn and cook for 30 seconds on the other side. Transfer fish to a roasting pan and roast at 180C for 5-6 minutes or until tender. Remove from oven and rest in a warm place for 2 minutes.

Meanwhile, cook noodles according to directions on packet, then drain.

Heat stock in a saucepan, add ginger, carrot, mushroom and half the green onion and simmer for 2 minutes, then season with soy sauce and rice wine.

Divide noodles among 6 bowls, spoon stock mixture over and top with fish and remaining green onion. Pass steamed asian greens with oyster sauce separately (recipe follows).

STEAMED ASIAN GREENS WITH OYSTER SAUCE

1 bunch baby bok choy,
 leaves separated and halved
1 bunch choy sum, trimmed and halved
1 tablespoon peanut oil
1 clove of garlic, finely chopped
2 tablespoons oyster sauce
1/3 cup chicken stock (see basic recipes)
1 teaspoon sesame oil

Place bok choy and choy sum in a large bamboo steamer. Place covered steamer over a wok of boiling water and steam for 5-8 minutes or until vegetables are tender.

Meanwhile, heat peanut oil in a small saucepan, add garlic and cook over medium heat for 30 seconds, then add remaining ingredients and bring to the boil. Pour stock mixture over vegetables and serve immediately.

wine: Tunnel Hill Pinot Noir, Yarra Valley, Vic. Pinot noir may not be the best-selling red wine variety in the country, but when it comes to matching wine with food it's a star. The Tunnel Hill pinot, made by TarraWarra, has sweet strawberry, raspberry and cherry fruit flavours and, with soft tannins and a fresh acid, it's a natural with this Asian seafood dish.

MANDARIN JELLIES WITH MELON

20g gelatine leaves
800ml strained mandarin juice
 (about 16 mandarins)
2 tablespoons caster sugar
100ml mandarin-flavoured vodka
2 oranges, segmented

MELON IN SPICED
VERJUICE SYRUP

1 cup verjuice
75g (1/3 cup) caster sugar
2 whole star anise
2 cinnamon sticks
400g rockmelon, cut into 2cm pieces
400g honeydew melon,
 cut into 2cm pieces

Soak gelatine leaves in cold water for 2-3 minutes or until soft. Drain and squeeze out excess water.

Combine mandarin juice and sugar in a saucepan and stir over low heat until sugar dissolves. Remove from heat and stir in drained gelatine sheets and vodka and mix well. Place orange segments in the base of six 125ml dariole moulds and spoon over enough mandarin liquid to just cover fruit, then refrigerate for 45 minutes or until firm. Pour remaining jelly mixture into moulds, then cover and refrigerate for 2-3 hours or overnight.

For melon in spiced verjuice syrup, combine verjuice, 1/2 cup water, sugar, star anise and cinnamon sticks in a small saucepan and stir over low heat until sugar dissolves. Increase heat and simmer until reduced by half. Remove from heat and cool to room temperature. Pour syrup over combined melon, then cover and refrigerate for 2 hours for flavours to develop.

Place jellies in warm water for 5 seconds, then turn out onto 6 plates and serve with melon in spiced verjuice syrup spooned to one side.

wine: Brown Brothers Moscato, Milawa, Vic. Moscato is made from early-picked white muscat grapes which are fermented until only half the sugars have been converted into alcohol. The result is a fresh, slightly sweet, intensely grapey wine with a refreshing sparkle. As a bonus, it's low in alcohol, so a second bottle is almost mandatory.

MANDARIN JELLIES WITH MELON

vegetarian indian banquet

menu serves 8

vegetable samosas

potato and split-pea curry

stir-fried beans with red capsicum

mustard-seed, eggplant and tomato curry

pilau

tomato and coriander sambal

coconut and banana raita

pistachio ice-cream with spiced dates

time planner

one day ahead: keep covered in refrigerator

- prepare vegetable filling for samosas
- cook potato and split-pea curry
- marinate spiced dates
- make pistachio ice-cream: keep covered in freezer

on the day

- prepare pastry and rest, degorge eggplant
- fill samosas
- cook eggplant curry and pilau
- prepare tomato sambal and banana raita
- deep-fry samosas and serve
- reheat potato and split-pea curry and serve
with other curry, pilau, sambal and raita
- serve pistachio ice-cream and spiced dates

VEGETABLE SAMOSAS

600g (4 cups) plain flour
2 teaspoons salt
1/2 cup vegetable oil
Vegetable oil, extra, for deep-frying
Mango chutney, to serve

VEGETABLE FILLING
350g sebago potatoes, scrubbed
1 tablespoon vegetable oil
1 small onion, finely chopped
2 cloves of garlic, chopped
2 teaspoons grated ginger
1 teaspoon ground cumin
Pinch of ground chillies
1 1/2 teaspoons ground coriander
1/2 teaspoon ground turmeric
2 teaspoons garam masala
60g (1/2 cup) fresh or frozen peas,
    blanched in boiling, salted water
    until just tender, then drained
150g cauliflower florets, chopped,
    then blanched in boiling water
    for 2 minutes and drained
1 1/2 tablespoons lemon juice
1/4 cup chopped coriander

For vegetable filling, cook potatoes in boiling, salted water until tender. Drain and cool, then peel and cut into 1cm pieces.

Heat oil in a saucepan, add onion, garlic and ginger and cook over medium heat for 3-4 minutes. Add spices and cook for another 2-3 minutes or until fragrant. Add blanched peas and cauliflower, potato, lemon juice and 1 tablespoon water and stir over medium heat for 3-4 minutes or until well combined. Season generously with salt and cracked black pepper and stir in coriander. Remove from heat and cool.

Sift flour and salt into a bowl, add oil and 1 cup warm water and mix until well combined and a soft dough forms. Knead dough on a lightly floured surface for 5-10 minutes or until smooth and elastic. Cover with plastic wrap and rest at room temperature for 1 hour.

Cut pastry in half, then roll out one half on a lightly floured surface until 3mm thick. Using a 12cm round biscuit cutter, cut out rounds. Place 1 heaped tablespoon of vegetable filling on one half of each round. Fold the other half over to enclose filling and pinch pastry edge over to seal. Repeat with remaining pastry and filling.

Deep-fry samosas, in batches, in hot vegetable oil, turning once, for 3-4 minutes or until golden. Drain on absorbent paper. Serve warm with mango chutney.

Makes about 16.

Indian vegetarian is vegetarian brought to genius level. The rich flavours, varying textures and glorious spice fragrances of a meal like this add up to one of the most adventurous and satisfying ways you can eat.

VEGETABLE SAMOSAS

MUSTARD-SEED, EGGPLANT AND TOMATO CURRY

POTATO AND SPLIT-PEA CURRY

1/4 cup ghee
1 1/2 teaspoons brown mustard seeds
1 teaspoon fenugreek seeds,
    lightly crushed
2 teaspoons grated ginger
2 cloves of garlic, crushed
2 teaspoons ground coriander
1/2 teaspoon ground turmeric
1 x 400g can whole tomatoes,
    drained and coarsely chopped
150g (3/4 cup) yellow split peas
1kg desirée potatoes,
    peeled and cut into 2cm pieces
2 teaspoons salt
1/3 cup chopped coriander
1 teaspoon garam masala
1 1/2 tablespoons lime juice

Heat ghee in a saucepan, add seeds, ginger and garlic and cook over medium heat for 2 minutes. Add ground coriander and turmeric and cook for another minute or until fragrant. Stir in tomato, split peas and 3 cups water, bring to the boil and simmer for 15 minutes or until peas are almost tender. Add potato and salt and simmer for another 25 minutes or until potato and peas are tender. Stir in remaining ingredients and season to taste with cracked black pepper.

STIR-FRIED BEANS WITH RED CAPSICUM

2 tablespoons vegetable oil
2 teaspoons cumin seeds
1 onion, chopped
1 1/2 tablespoons mild curry paste
2 tablespoons chopped coriander
1 large red banana capsicum, sliced
250g beans, trimmed
250g roman beans, trimmed
1 tablespoon sugar
1 1/2 teaspoons sambal ulek, or to taste

Heat oil in a wok or large frying pan, add cumin seeds and cook for 30 seconds, then add onion and curry paste and stir over medium heat for 2-3 minutes. Add coriander, banana capsicum and beans and cook for 1 minute. Stir in sugar and sambal ulek and stir-fry over high heat for 3-4 minutes or until beans are just tender. Season to taste and serve immediately.

MUSTARD-SEED, EGGPLANT AND TOMATO CURRY

600g eggplant, cut into 1cm-thick slices
Mustard-seed or vegetable oil
6 shallots, sliced
1 tablespoon grated ginger
1 1/2 tablespoons brown mustard seeds
30 curry leaves
1 teaspoon ground turmeric
1/2 teaspoon ground chillies
1 teaspoon ground coriander
500g tomatoes, chopped
1 1/2 tablespoons tomato paste

Layer eggplant in a colander, sprinkling each layer with salt and stand for 30 minutes. Rinse well and pat dry with absorbent paper, then cut into 2cm pieces.

Heat 2 tablespoons mustard-seed or vegetable oil in a wok and cook half the eggplant over high heat until browned. Drain on absorbent paper. Heat another 2 tablespoons oil and repeat with remaining eggplant until browned. Remove from wok.

Heat 1 tablespoon mustard-seed or vegetable oil in same wok, add shallot, ginger, mustard seeds and curry leaves and cook over medium heat for 5 minutes. Add spices, tomato and tomato paste and cook for 2 minutes, then add eggplant, season to taste and simmer over medium heat for 5 minutes or until eggplant is tender and tomato is pulpy.

PILAU

500g (2½ cups) basmati rice
2 tablespoons ghee
1 tablespoon vegetable oil
2 onions, thinly sliced
110g (¾ cup) whole raw cashews
40g (¼ cup) whole blanched almonds
8 cardamom pods, lightly crushed
4 cloves
1 cinnamon stick
8 black peppercorns
½ teaspoon saffron threads,
   soaked in 1 tablespoon
   boiling water for 10 minutes
2 teaspoons salt
Roasted unsalted cashews, to serve

Wash rice in a sieve under running water until water runs clear.

Heat ghee and oil in a large saucepan, add onion and cook over medium heat for 5 minutes. Add nuts and spices and cook for another 3-4 minutes or until spices are fragrant and onion is just golden. Stir in rice and cook for 2 minutes until lightly roasted.

Add saffron mixture, 1 litre boiling water and salt, bring to the boil, then reduce heat and cook, covered, over very low heat for 15-20 minutes or until liquid has been absorbed and rice is tender. Remove from heat and stand, covered, for 10 minutes. Serve sprinkled with roasted unsalted cashews.

TOMATO AND CORIANDER SAMBAL

4 small tomatoes
1 small spanish onion,
   thinly sliced lengthwise
¼ cup chopped coriander
2 tablespoons flat-leaf parsley leaves
¼ cup lime juice
½ teaspoon cayenne
1 teaspoon roasted cumin seeds,
   lightly crushed in a mortar and pestle

Cut tomatoes into thin wedges and place in a glass or ceramic bowl. Add remaining ingredients, season to taste and stand for 1 hour for flavours to develop.

COCONUT AND BANANA RAITA

2 firm, ripe bananas, peeled and sliced
1 tablespoon lemon juice
1/3 cup Greek-style plain yoghurt
2 tablespoons desiccated coconut
1/2 teaspoon sugar

Drizzle banana with lemon juice. Combine yoghurt, coconut and sugar, stir into banana mixture and stand for 1 hour for flavours to develop.

PISTACHIO ICE-CREAM WITH SPICED DATES

Two 375ml cans of evaporated milk can be substituted for the milk. Omit the evaporation stage and start where you add the sugar and cream, adding the cardamom pods at this stage. Discard the pods before pouring the mixture into dariole moulds.

2 litres milk
10 cardamom pods
75g (1/3 cup) caster sugar
1/3 cup pouring cream
110g (3/4 cup) shelled unsalted
    pistachios, roasted and chopped
Roasted and chopped pistachios,
    extra, to serve

SPICED DATES

1 cinnamon stick
4 cardamom pods
110g (1/2 cup) caster sugar
Pinch of saffron threads
12 fresh dates, seeded
    and quartered lengthwise

For spiced dates, combine all ingredients, except dates, with 1 cup water in a saucepan and simmer over low heat until reduced by one third and syrupy. Pour warm syrup over dates and cool to room temperature, then refrigerate until cold.

Combine milk and cardamom in a saucepan, bring just to the boil and simmer over medium heat, stirring regularly to incorporate skin on surface, for about 1 1/2 hours or until reduced to 800ml. Strain milk mixture, discarding solids.

Return reduced milk to a clean saucepan, add sugar, cream and pistachios and stir until heated through. Remove from heat and cool to room temperature. Pour mixture into eight 125ml-capacity dariole moulds, cover with foil and freeze for 3 hours or until firm.

Run a knife around side of moulds, turn out onto plates, sprinkle with extra pistachios and serve immediately with spiced dates and syrup.

wines: Here are some suggestions for what to drink with these dishes. **Lowe Family Semillon, Hunter Valley, NSW.** Sweet, spicy dishes work best with riesling. The more savoury, complex and earthy spices of India combine best with the fresh, savoury and herbal flavours of a young semillon. Winemaker David Lowe is a master with this variety. **Yering Station Pinot Noir Rosé ED, Yarra Valley, Vic.** Many rosés are white wines with a slash of red for colour – not this excellent Yering Station rosé which is made from pinot noir fruit sourced from vines too young to be used for their red wines. Fresh, crisp and dry, it is a wonderful food wine. **Frangelico Liqueur, Italy.** This hazelnut liqueur is the perfect drink to partner the intense nuttiness of the pistachios, the earthy sweetness of the dates and the spiciness of the syrup. Serve it chilled or over ice.

simple sunday dinner

WARM AVOCADO, GRAPEFRUIT AND SCALLOP SALAD

1 tablespoon lime juice
Olive oil
2 teaspoons walnut oil
150g mesclun
2 avocados, peeled, seeded and sliced
2 pink grapefruit, peeled, segmented
  and coarsely chopped
20 scallops, roe removed
1 egg white, lightly beaten
55g (1/3 cup) cornmeal,
  seasoned to taste

Whisk lime juice, 2 tablespoons olive oil, walnut oil and a pinch of sugar, then season to taste. Combine mesclun, avocado, grapefruit and dressing, toss gently and divide among 4 plates.

Toss scallops in egg white, then drain. Dust coated scallops in seasoned cornmeal and shake away excess. Heat 1 1/2 tablespoons olive oil in a heavy-based frying pan and cook scallops, in batches, for 45-60 seconds on each side until golden and just tender. Serve salad topped with scallops.

wine: Reynolds Yarraman Semillon, Hunter Valley, NSW.

PORK CUTLETS WITH CORN AND SAGE PANCAKES

4 pork loin cutlets (about 200g each)
1 clove of garlic, flattened
1 tablespoon finely chopped
  sage leaves
Olive oil
Wilted spinach tossed with a little
  balsamic vinegar, to serve

CORN AND SAGE PANCAKES

150g (1 cup) self-raising flour
1/4 teaspoon bicarbonate of soda
3/4 cup buttermilk
2 cobs of corn, blanched
  and kernels removed
2 eggs
25g (1/3 cup) grated parmesan
1 tablespoon finely chopped sage
50g butter, chopped

For corn and sage pancakes, sift flour, bicarbonate of soda and a pinch of salt into a bowl. Whisk buttermilk, corn kernels, eggs, parmesan and sage in another bowl until well combined, then gradually whisk into flour mixture to form a thick batter. Melt a little butter in a non-stick frying pan, add 1/4 cupfuls of pancake batter, in batches, and cook over low heat for 2-3 minutes on each side until golden. Cover pancakes and keep warm.

Rub pork with garlic, then discard garlic. Sprinkle pork with sage and season to taste. Heat a little olive oil in a large frying pan and cook pork, in batches, over medium heat until well browned. Transfer to a roasting pan and roast at 200C for 5-10 minutes or until tender. Rest pork, covered, in a warm place for 5 minutes. Spoon spinach onto plates and top with pork cutlets and pancakes.

wine: Orlando St Hilary Chardonnay, Padthaway, SA.

SELF-SAUCING CHOCOLATE AND ESPRESSO PUDDING

225g (1 1/2 cups) self-raising flour
35g (1/3 cup) Dutch cocoa
220g (1 cup) caster sugar
50g butter, melted
1 egg, lightly beaten
180ml milk
75g dark couverture chocolate
  (50% cocoa solids), chopped
2 cups hot espresso coffee
Vanilla ice-cream or thick cream,
  to serve

Sift flour and cocoa into a bowl, then stir in sugar. Add butter and combined egg and milk and mix well. Stir in chocolate and spoon mixture into a greased 2.5-litre-capacity soufflé dish. Pour hot espresso coffee over pudding, place dish on a baking tray and bake at 180C for 40 minutes or until puffed and firm to the touch. Serve immediately with vanilla ice-cream or thick cream.

wine: Buller Classic Tokay, Rutherglen, Vic.

When the weather is wintry, it's great to be inside eating crisp-crusted seafood on a fabulous salad, rich pork and pancakes and a proper pudding with the beloved flavours of chocolate and coffee.

PORK CUTLETS WITH CORN AND SAGE PANCAKES

informal dinner party

menu serves 6

antipasto of white-bean purée and salad,

swiss-brown mushroom and shallot frittata,

wilted salad with roasted hazelnuts and goat's cheese

poached chicken with winter vegetables and tarragon pistou

orange and oat biscuits with macerated muscatels and camembert

pear clafoutis

time planner

in advance

- macerate muscatels: make 1 week ahead
- orange and oat biscuits can be made 3 days ahead: keep in airtight container

one day ahead: keep covered in refrigerator

- prepare white-bean purée and bake frittata
- poach chicken, cool in poaching liquid
- prepare tarragon pistou

on the day

- prepare vegetables and cook soup
- roast pears and cook clafoutis
- wilt radicchio and rocket, serve with goat's cheese, hazelnuts and prosciutto on antipasto plate with bean purée and salad and frittata
- add chicken to soup and serve with pistou
- serve orange oat biscuits with macerated muscatels and cheese
- serve warm clafoutis with mascarpone

ANTIPASTO

The following three dishes can be served on individual plates or on one large plate placed in the middle of the table.

WHITE-BEAN PUREE AND SALAD

300g (1 1/2 cups) dried white beans,
   soaked in water overnight
Juice of 2 lemons
2 cloves of garlic, finely chopped
1/3 cup Greek-style plain yoghurt
Extra virgin olive oil
Grated rind of 1 lemon
1 tablespoon lemon juice, extra
100g small black olives
1/4 cup drained and rinsed capers
2 tablespoons chopped oregano leaves

Cook white beans in simmering water for about 50 minutes or until tender. Drain and cool to room temperature. Reserve 1 1/3 cups whole beans and process remaining beans, lemon juice, garlic, yoghurt and 1 tablespoon extra virgin olive oil in a food processor until smooth. Season to taste.

Combine reserved beans with lemon rind and extra juice, olives, capers, oregano and 2 tablespoons extra virgin olive oil and season to taste.

Spread white-bean purée onto a plate and spoon white-bean salad over. Serve at room temperature.

SWISS-BROWN MUSHROOM AND SHALLOT FRITTATA

2 tablespoons olive oil
200g shallots, chopped
200g swiss-brown mushrooms, sliced
8 eggs, lightly beaten
50g parmesan, grated
35g (1/2 cup) fresh breadcrumbs

Heat olive oil in a large frying pan, stir in shallot, cover and cook over low heat for 10 minutes or until soft. Add mushroom and stir-fry over medium heat for 3-4 minutes or until mushroom is just soft. Cool.

Combine mushroom mixture, eggs, parmesan and breadcrumbs in a large bowl, season to taste and mix well. Pour mixture into a baking-paper-lined 26cm ovenproof frying pan and bake at 190C for 20 minutes or until just set. Place frittata under a hot grill and cook until top is golden. Cool and serve cut into wedges.

This is cheerful, hearty food that can be eaten with a fork and a spoon, so you have the option of serving it anywhere pleasant and relaxing.

WILTED SALAD WITH ROASTED HAZELNUTS AND GOAT'S CHEESE; SWISS-BROWN MUSHROOM AND SHALLOT FRITTATA; WHITE-BEAN PUREE AND SALAD

POACHED CHICKEN WITH WINTER
VEGETABLES AND TARRAGON PISTOU

WILTED SALAD WITH ROASTED HAZELNUTS AND GOAT'S CHEESE

1 radicchio, tough outer leaves removed
1 large bunch of rocket, trimmed
1/2 cup verjuice or chicken stock
    (see basic recipes), flavoured
    with a little lemon juice
100g (2/3 cup) hazelnuts, roasted,
    skins removed and coarsely chopped
150g goat's cheese, crumbled
6 slices prosciutto

Separate radicchio leaves and tear into large pieces. Heat a non-stick frying pan, add radicchio, rocket and verjuice or stock and stir-fry over medium heat until leaves are just wilted. Transfer to a plate, pour pan juices over, sprinkle with hazelnuts and goat's cheese and season to taste. Serve with prosciutto.

wine: Fermoy Estate Semillon, Margaret River, WA. An antipasto plate needs a wine that has good weight of flavour without being too fruity. The wine also needs structure without being oaky and should show freshness without being lightweight. This lemony fresh Fermoy semillon meets all these criteria.

POACHED CHICKEN WITH WINTER VEGETABLES AND TARRAGON PISTOU

1 teaspoon salt
1 x 1.8kg free-range chicken
1 onion, quartered
10 black peppercorns
1/4 cup olive oil
2 cloves of garlic, finely chopped
3 large leeks, white part only,
    cut into 1cm slices
2 bulbs of fennel, halved,
    cored and sliced
700g kipfler potatoes, scrubbed
    and cut into large chunks
900g large vine-ripened tomatoes,
    peeled, seeded and coarsely chopped
1 cup verjuice or reserved chicken stock
Tarragon pistou (see basic recipes),
    to serve

Rub salt all over chicken, then place chicken, breast side down, in a large saucepan and add onion, peppercorns and enough water to cover. Bring to a simmer and poach for 1-1¼ hours or until chicken is cooked through. Cool in poaching liquid.

Remove chicken from poaching liquid and strain stock into a large saucepan. Bring stock to the boil and boil until reduced to 2 litres. Remove flesh from chicken, discarding skin and bones, and

cut into large, bite-sized pieces.

Heat oil in a large saucepan, add garlic, leek, fennel and potato and stir to coat well. Cover and cook, stirring occasionally, over low heat for 30 minutes. Add 1 litre of reduced chicken stock (reserve remaining stock), tomato and verjuice or reserved stock, bring to the boil, then reduce heat and simmer, partly covered, for 30-35 minutes or until vegetables are tender. Season to taste, add chicken and simmer gently over low heat for 5 minutes or until chicken is heated through. Serve in warm bowls topped with a spoonful of tarragon pistou.

wine: Tamar Ridge Pinot Noir, Tamar Valley, Tas. Tasmanian pinot is generally softer, fleshier and more elegant than many of its mainland compatriots, the banks of the Tamar River being ideal for its cultivation. Upfront and friendly, this one has lots of cherry and raspberry fruit flavours with gentle oak handling and a tight finish.

PEAR CLAFOUTIS

ORANGE AND OAT BISCUITS WITH MACERATED MUSCATELS AND CAMEMBERT

110g (1/2 cup) caster sugar
Julienned rind of 2 oranges
175g wholemeal plain flour
50g fine oatmeal
1 tablespoon brown sugar
1 teaspoon baking powder
120g soft butter, chopped
1/2 teaspoon pure orange oil
Camembert, to serve

MACERATED MUSCATELS
300g dried muscatels
2 cinnamon sticks
Grated rind of 1 orange
Verdelho or madeira, to cover

For macerated muscatels, combine muscatels, cinnamon sticks and rind in a glass jar and cover with verdelho or madeira. Seal jar and macerate for at least 1 week before using.

Combine 1 cup water and caster sugar in a small saucepan and stir over low heat until sugar dissolves. Add orange rind and cook over medium heat, without stirring, for 15 minutes or until rind softens and caramelises slightly. Cool slightly. Using a slotted spoon, remove rind and chop finely; reserve syrup. Process flour, oatmeal, brown sugar, baking powder, candied rind and 1/2 teaspoon salt in a food processor until just combined. Add butter and process until mixture resembles breadcrumbs. Add 1 tablespoon reserved syrup and orange oil and process until mixture forms a ball. Wrap in plastic wrap and refrigerate for 30 minutes.

Roll out dough on a lightly floured surface until 6mm thick and, using a 5cm round biscuit cutter, cut out shapes. Place biscuits on baking-paper-lined oven trays and bake at 180C for 15 minutes or until pale golden. Stand biscuits for 5 minutes on oven trays before transferring to a wire rack to cool.

Serve with macerated muscatels and wedges of camembert.

Makes about 25 biscuits.

PEAR CLAFOUTIS

6 ripe beurre bosc pears, peeled,
    cored and each cut into 4-6 pieces
    (depending on size)
50g (1/4 cup) brown sugar
2 tablespoons lemon juice
40ml Poire William or brandy
110g (3/4 cup) plain flour, sifted
160g (1 cup) pure icing sugar, sifted
1 1/2 cups milk
1 cup pouring cream
4 eggs
Icing sugar, extra, for dusting

MASCARPONE
250g mascarpone
20ml Poire William or brandy
1 tablespoon pure icing sugar

For mascarpone, combine all ingredients in a bowl and whisk until soft peaks form.

Place pear in a large ovenproof dish, sprinkle with sugar and pour lemon juice and pear liqueur or brandy over. Stir gently to combine. Roast pear at 180C, turning once, for 30 minutes or until very tender. Drain, reserve pan juices and cool pear to room temperature.

Combine flour and icing sugar in the bowl of an electric mixer. Combine milk, cream and 1/2 cup reserved pan juices in a jug. With mixer on medium speed, gradually add milk mixture and beat until smooth. Add eggs, one at a time, beating well after each, then beat until batter is smooth. Place pear in a well-greased 8-cup-capacity shallow ceramic baking dish. Pour batter over and bake at 180C for 50 minutes or until clafoutis is set and golden brown. Dust with icing sugar and serve immediately with mascarpone.

wine: Buller Fine Old Malmsey Madeira, Rutherglen, Vic. Madeira is often derided as old-fashioned, yet it offers lots of food-friendly characters a weight and intensity from the fortification and a richness from its time in oak. The finish is dry enough to pair with both the cheese and the pear.

simple dinner party

BLUE-CHEESE GOUGERE

40g unsalted butter, chopped
75g (1/2 cup) plain flour
2 eggs
40g firm blue cheese, crumbled
Flaked sea salt, to serve

Combine butter and 1/2 cup water in a small, heavy-based saucepan and bring to the boil. Add flour and stir vigorously until mixture thickens and pulls away from side of pan. Remove from heat and whisk in eggs, one at a time, beating well after each. Add cheese and cracked black pepper to taste and mix gently. Spoon teaspoonfuls of mixture onto baking-paper-lined oven trays. Bake at 200C for 10 minutes, reduce temperature to 190C and bake for another 5-8 minutes or until golden and puffed. Serve immediately sprinkled with flaked sea salt.

Makes about 22.
wine: Tulloch Verdelho, Hunter Valley, NSW.

POACHED FILLET OF BEEF WITH GRILLED WITLOF AND HORSERADISH CREAM

2 teaspoons grated fresh horseradish
    or bottled horseradish
1/3 cup light sour cream
1 x 800g eye fillet of beef
3 cups veal stock (see basic recipes)
3 cups chicken stock
    (see basic recipes)
600g orange sweet potato,
    peeled and cut into 2cm pieces
4 witlof, halved
Olive oil

Combine horseradish and sour cream and season to taste.

Tie beef with string at 3cm intervals to form a neat shape, season liberally with sea salt and cracked black pepper and refrigerate for 1 hour. Place beef in the bottom of a large saucepan to fit snugly, cover with combined veal and chicken stock and bring to the boil. Reduce heat and poach gently for 20 minutes. Remove beef from pan and rest in a warm place for 10 minutes. Bring 2 cups stock back to the boil, skim, reduce by half, strain through a fine sieve and season to taste.

Meanwhile, place sweet potato on an oven tray, brush lightly with oil and roast at 200C for 25-30 minutes or until browned and tender. Place witlof on an oven tray, brush with a little oil and grill on both sides until well browned.

Place sliced beef on warm plates, drizzle with a little poaching liquid and serve with grilled witlof, roasted sweet potato and horseradish cream.
wine: Henschke Keyneton Estate, Eden Valley, SA.

RHUBARB AND STRAWBERRY COMPOTE WITH SHORTBREAD

20g butter
2 tablespoons honey
1 cinnamon stick
4 sticks of rhubarb,
    trimmed and cut into 4cm pieces
250g strawberries, hulled and halved

SHORTBREAD
125g soft butter, chopped
80g (1/2 cup) icing sugar, sifted
150g (1 cup) plain flour

For shortbread, using an electric mixer, beat butter until pale, then add icing sugar and beat until creamy. Stir in sifted flour and mix to combine. Roll level tablespoons of mixture into balls and place on an oven tray. Press down with the back of a fork. Bake at 180C for 10-12 minutes until golden. Cool on tray for 10 minutes until firm, then transfer to a wire rack to cool.

Combine butter, honey, 2 tablespoons water and cinnamon stick in a frying pan and cook over medium heat until butter and honey dissolve. Add rhubarb and simmer, stirring occasionally, for 5 minutes. Add strawberries and simmer for 2 minutes. Remove cinnamon stick before serving compote with shortbread.

Makes about 15 shortbreads. Will keep in an airtight container for 1 week.
wine: Coriole Botrytis Chenin Blanc, McLaren Vale, SA.

Poaching is an unusual way to cook beef fillet, but it gives rosy slices of unrivalled succulence and flavour. Serve the gougère with pre-dinner drinks, then sit down when the beef and vegetables are ready.

vegetarian dinner party

CHICKPEA FRITTERS WITH AVOCADO TOPPING

200g (1 cup) chickpeas,
    soaked in cold water overnight
3 green onions, finely chopped
1 clove of garlic, finely chopped
1 teaspoon ground cumin
1/4 cup chopped coriander
Vegetable oil, for deep-frying
Sweet chilli sauce, to serve

AVOCADO TOPPING

1 avocado
2 teaspoons lime juice
1 teaspoon sweet chilli sauce

Drain chickpeas well and process in a food processor with remaining ingredients until smooth, then season to taste. Roll level tablespoons of mixture into patties, then cover and refrigerate for 30 minutes. Deep-fry patties, in batches, in hot vegetable oil until browned and crisp. Drain on absorbent paper.

For avocado topping, process all ingredients in a food processor until smooth, then season to taste.

Serve warm chickpea fritters with avocado topping and drizzle with a little sweet chilli sauce.

Makes about 20.

wine: Domaine Chatelain Pouilly Fumé, Loire Valley, France. Pouilly Fumé is made from sauvignon blanc, although it is poles apart from the passionfruit and gooseberry flavours of Australian sauvignons and the fresh, grassy styles produced in New Zealand. Pouilly Fumé has finely balanced savoury flavours that will complement the nuttiness of the chickpeas, while its rapier-like acidity will cut through the richness of the avocado.

time planner

one day ahead: keep covered in refrigerator

- prepare chickpea fritters
- prepare filling for ravioli
- prepare eggplant and capsicum for torte
- cook figs in cinnamon syrup
- bake meringue discs: keep in airtight container
- bake and fill yoyos: keep in airtight container

on the day

- assemble ravioli
- finish torte and bake
- prepare avocado topping, deep-fry fritters and serve
- cook ravioli, prepare sauce and serve
- prepare mushroom salad and serve with torte
- serve meringues with figs in syrup, followed by yoyos

Elegant, sophisticated – and vegetarian. This dinner party welcomes guests with drinks and crisp little fritters, moves to the table for delicate ravioli and is crowned with a delicious savoury torte. Finish with figs on mascarpone and nutty meringue, and linger over coffee and biscuits.

CHICKPEA FRITTERS WITH AVOCADO TOPPING

SPINACH AND SWEET-POTATO RAVIOLI

SPINACH AND SWEET-POTATO RAVIOLI

600g orange sweet potato,
    peeled and chopped
1/2 bunch spinach, washed and sliced
100g ricotta, drained
Pinch of nutmeg, to taste
2 x 275g packets gow gee wrappers
1 egg, lightly beaten
    with 1 tablespoon water

SAUCE
200g butter, chopped
4 cloves of garlic, quartered
80g (1/2 cup) pinenuts
1/3 cup lemon juice
2 tablespoons each of chopped chives,
    basil and flat-leaf parsley

Place sweet potato in the top of a steamer, cover and steam over boiling water for 10-15 minutes or until tender, then transfer to a plate. Add spinach to steamer and steam for 3-4 minutes until just wilted; squeeze out excess moisture.

Using a potato masher, mash sweet potato with ricotta and season with salt, pepper and nutmeg to taste. Stir in steamed spinach and mix well. Place 6 gow gee wrappers on a floured surface and place 1 heaped tablespoon of sweet-potato mixture in the centre of each. Brush edges of pastry with egg mixture, top with another wrapper and press edges together firmly. Repeat with remaining wrappers, sweet-potato mixture and egg wash.

Cook ravioli, in batches, in simmering, salted water for 2-3 minutes until tender. Remove with a slotted spoon and drain.

Meanwhile, for sauce, add butter, garlic and pinenuts to a deep frying pan and stir over low heat until butter melts, then cook for 1-2 minutes or until pinenuts are lightly browned. Remove garlic and continue to cook pinenuts over medium heat until butter begins to froth and brown. Add lemon juice and herbs and stir until heated through. Divide ravioli among 8 plates and spoon sauce over.

wine: Caves du Turkheim Tokay Pinot Gris Reserve, Alsace, France. Historically (and confusingly), pinot gris was called tokay in Alsace – this label includes both names for good measure. An intensely flavoured, spicy and potent white wine, it has the backbone, weight and power to partner the richness of the sweet potato and the earthiness of the spinach.

EGGPLANT AND CAPSICUM TORTE

4 eggplant (about 1.2kg), sliced
    lengthwise into 5mm-thick slices
Olive oil
2 red capsicum, quartered
8 eggs
600ml pomodoro
1/2 cup torn basil leaves
300g gruyère, grated

Brush eggplant with a little olive oil and char-grill, in batches, over high heat on both sides until browned and tender. Place in a single layer on absorbent paper, top with more paper, then repeat layering, top with more paper and press down gently to remove excess moisture.

Place capsicum, skin side down, on an oven tray and grill under high heat for 8 minutes. Turn over and grill for another 8-10 minutes until skin is blistered and blackened. Place in a paper bag and stand for 20 minutes, then peel. Place peeled capsicum on absorbent paper in a single layer, top with more absorbent paper and press down gently to remove excess moisture.

Whisk eggs well and season to taste.

Bring pomodoro to the boil in a saucepan and simmer over medium heat for 10-15 minutes or until thick and reduced by about one third.

Place eggplant, overlapping, in a circular pattern over base of an oiled, base-lined 24cm cake tin. Place more eggplant slices around side of pan, allowing eggplant to overhang side. Spoon one third of the reduced pomodoro over eggplant, scatter with one third of the basil and sprinkle with one third of the cheese, then pour over one third of the egg mixture. Repeat with half the remaining pomodoro, basil and cheese, then top with roasted capsicum and pour over half the remaining egg. Repeat layering once more and pour over remaining egg. Finish with a layer of eggplant, then fold in overhanging eggplant. Bake at 180C for 70-80 minutes or until firm to touch. Stand torte for 30-40 minutes, then run a knife around edge of tin and turn out. Serve wedges of torte with mushroom and radicchio salad (recipe follows).

wine: Guigal Côtes du Rhône, Rhone Valley, France. This soft and delicious red wine is made from grenache, shiraz and mourvèdre. Although quite rich and flavoursome, its savoury characters are a good match for the eggplant and for the mushroom in the salad. The bitterness of the radicchio will add a piquancy to the soft tannins of the red.

MUSHROOM AND RADICCHIO SALAD

2 cloves of garlic, finely chopped
2/3 cup olive oil
2 sprigs of rosemary
1/4 cup sherry vinegar
2 teaspoons seeded mustard
600g flat mushrooms (about 6-7),
    peeled and stalks removed
1 bunch of rocket, trimmed
1 head of radicchio,
    leaves separated and torn

Combine garlic, oil and rosemary in a small saucepan and cook over low heat for 5 minutes or until garlic just begins to brown. Remove from heat, discard rosemary and carefully whisk in vinegar and mustard. Place mushrooms, skin side up, on an oven tray, brush with a little dressing and grill under medium heat for 2-3 minutes. Turn mushrooms over, brush with more dressing and grill for another 3-4 minutes or until tender. Combine thickly sliced mushrooms, rocket and radicchio in a large salad bowl, pour any remaining dressing over and toss to combine.

PECAN MERINGUE DISCS WITH FIGS IN CINNAMON SYRUP

4 egg whites
220g (1 cup) caster sugar
50g (1/2 cup) pecans, finely chopped
1/2 teaspoon ground cinnamon
400g mascarpone

FIGS IN CINNAMON SYRUP

1/2 cup light corn syrup
125ml dry white wine
110g (1/2 cup) caster sugar
1 cinnamon stick
24 dried figs (375g), hard tops removed

Beat egg whites with an electric mixer until soft peaks form, gradually add sugar 55g (1/4 cup) at a time, beating for 3-4 minutes after each addition or until sugar dissolves, then beat until thick and glossy. Fold in pecans and cinnamon and mix well. Spoon meringue into a piping bag fitted with a 1cm plain tube and pipe sixteen 7cm discs onto baking-paper-lined oven trays. Bake at 140C for 30 minutes, swap trays from top to bottom, and bake for another 30 minutes or until meringues are dry. Cool on trays.

For figs in cinnamon syrup, combine corn syrup, wine, sugar and cinnamon stick in a saucepan and stir over low heat until sugar dissolves, then simmer over medium heat for 5 minutes. Add figs to syrup and simmer for another 5-10 minutes or until syrup is slightly thick and golden.

Place a meringue disc on each plate, top with a spoonful of mascarpone and 3 figs, drizzle with syrup, then place another disc to the side.

wine: Château Filhot, Sauternes, France. Australian dessert wines often have too much fruit flavour and are too sweet to marry with many desserts. This classic Sauternes shows the restraint and the fresh acid structure typical of the region. The intense pear and apricot fruit flavours give sufficient richness to make this a perfect pairing.

ORANGE AND PASSIONFRUIT YOYOS

150g soft butter, chopped
75g (1/3 cup) caster sugar
2 teaspoons grated orange rind
200g (1 1/3 cups) plain flour
50g (1/3 cup) rice flour

PASSIONFRUIT BUTTER

30g soft butter
80g (1/2 cup) icing sugar
1 tablespoon passionfruit pulp

Beat butter, sugar and orange rind until light and fluffy. Stir in flours and, using a wooden spoon, mix until combined. Knead gently on a lightly floured surface until smooth. Roll walnut-sized pieces of dough into balls, place on greased baking trays and flatten with the back of a fork. Bake at 180C for 10-15 minutes or until crisp and golden. Stand for 5 minutes before transferring to a wire rack to cool.

For passionfruit butter, beat butter with a wooden spoon until pale and creamy, add half the icing sugar and beat until well combined. Add passionfruit pulp and remaining icing sugar and beat until well combined and fluffy. Spread passionfruit butter onto half the biscuits, then top with remaining biscuits.

Makes about 16.

simple celebration dinner

menu serves 8

bresaola and shaved fennel with croûtons

seared salmon with rocket and prawn mash

blood-orange and almond cake with rosewater cream

BRESAOLA AND SHAVED FENNEL WITH CROUTONS

250g thinly sliced bresaola
1 bulb of baby fennel, cored
    and thinly sliced on a mandolin
1 tablespoon truffle oil
1 tablespoon lemon juice
50g Parmigiano Reggiano, flaked
Thinly sliced toasted ciabatta, to serve

Place bresaola on a large plate in overlapping slices and sprinkle with fennel. Drizzle with combined truffle oil and lemon juice, sprinkle with parmesan and season to taste with sea salt and cracked black pepper. Serve with toasted ciabatta.
wine: St Hallet Semillon Select, Barossa Valley, SA.

SEARED SALMON WITH ROCKET AND PRAWN MASH

1.5kg sebago potatoes,
    peeled and quartered
4 cloves of garlic, crushed
Olive oil
16 medium uncooked prawns,
    peeled, deveined and chopped
1/2 cup lemon juice
2 cups rocket leaves
8 salmon fillets
    (about 120g each), skinned
Fried capers, to serve

Cook potato in boiling, salted water until tender, then drain and mash with garlic and 1/3 cup olive oil.

Heat 1/4 cup olive oil in a frying pan and stir prawns over high heat for 30 seconds until pink. Stir in 1/4 cup lemon juice and rocket and season to taste. Stir prawn mixture into mash and check seasoning.

Heat a little olive oil in a frying pan and cook salmon, in batches, over high heat on both sides until browned and just cooked.

Combine remaining lemon juice with 1/4 cup olive oil and season to taste. Serve salmon on a bed of mash, drizzle plate with oil mixture and sprinkle with fried capers and a little cracked black pepper.
wine: Diamond Valley Vineyards Blue Label Pinot Noir, Yarra Valley, Vic.

BLOOD-ORANGE AND ALMOND CAKE WITH ROSEWATER CREAM

6 eggs, separated
175g caster sugar
Grated rind and juice of 1 blood orange
175g ground almonds
70g (1 cup) day-old breadcrumbs

SYRUP

8 blood oranges
125g caster sugar
Squeeze of lemon juice, to taste

ROSEWATER CREAM

1 cup thick cream
1 tablespoon rosewater
1 tablespoon honey
1/2 teaspoon ground cardamom

Using an electric mixer, beat egg yolks, sugar, orange rind and juice until pale and thick, then stir in ground almonds and breadcrumbs (mixture will be very thick at this stage).

Separately, beat egg whites until stiff peaks just form. Add a spoonful of beaten egg white to loosen cake mixture, then gently fold through remaining egg white until just combined. Spoon mixture into a greased and floured base-lined 23cm springform pan and bake at 190C for 30-35 minutes (cover top of cake with foil if cake begins to over-brown) or until cake has risen and is springy to the touch. Remove cake from oven, cover tightly with foil and stand in pan for 5 minutes, then transfer to a wire rack to cool.

For syrup, squeeze juice from 4 oranges into a saucepan. Peel and slice remaining oranges. Add sugar to pan and stir over medium heat until sugar dissolves, then bring to the boil. Simmer syrup for 8 minutes, add orange slices and remove from heat. Cool slightly, then adjust syrup to taste with a little lemon juice.

Transfer cake to a plate with a lip. Using a skewer, spike top of cake all over. Spoon half the syrup over and top with orange slices.

For rosewater cream, beat all ingredients with an electric mixer until soft peaks form. Serve sliced cake warm or at room temperature with rosewater cream and remaining syrup.
wine: McWilliam's Mount Pleasant Madeira, Hunter Valley, NSW.

Here, luxury ingredients make a dinner that's special but easy. Bake the cake ahead of time, and the first-course salad and the salmon on its bed of wonderfully extravagant mash can be put together very quickly.

SEARED SALMON WITH ROCKET AND PRAWN MASH

elegant dinner party

menu serves 8

tiny noodle pancakes with spicy avocado and salmon roe

roasted chicken with braised leeks and soy and olive dressing

goat's cheese with apple wedges and oat biscuits

bitter-chocolate tart

GOAT'S CHEESE WITH APPLE WEDGES AND OAT BISCUITS

time planner

one day ahead: keep covered in refrigerator

• prepare soy and olive dressing

• bake chocolate tart

on the day

• prepare spicy avocado topping and pancake mixture

• roast chicken

• cook pancakes and serve

• braise vegetables and serve with chicken and dressing

• serve cheese with apple wedges and oat biscuits

• serve chocolate tart

TINY NOODLE PANCAKES WITH SPICY AVOCADO AND SALMON ROE

1 small avocado, peeled, stoned
   and finely chopped
1 tablespoon mango chutney
1/4 small spanish onion, finely chopped
1 teaspoon finely chopped basil
1/2 small tomato,
   seeded and finely chopped
1/2 fresh, small red chilli,
   seeded and finely chopped
1 tablespoon lime juice
2 tablespoons salmon roe, to serve

NOODLE PANCAKES
50g rice vermicelli noodles
1/2 sheet nori
140ml coconut cream
35g (1/4 cup) rice flour
2 egg whites
Peanut oil

For noodle pancakes, soak noodles in boiling water for about 5 minutes. Drain well, pat dry with absorbent paper and chop coarsely. Soak nori in warm water for 1 minute, drain and pat dry with absorbent paper, then slice into thin strips.

Combine coconut cream and rice flour and mix well. Stir in noodles and nori and season to taste with salt, pepper and a pinch of sugar. Whisk egg whites until soft peaks form and fold into noodle mixture in 2 batches. Heat a little peanut oil in a frying pan and cook scant tablespoons of noodle mixture, in batches, until brown, turning to brown other side. Drain on absorbent paper. Combine avocado and remaining ingredients, except salmon roe, and season to taste.

Serve noodle pancakes topped with spicy avocado and a little salmon roe.

Makes about 24.

wine: Chandon Vintage Brut Rosé, Yarra Valley, Vic. Pink sparkling wines gain their colour from the addition of a splash of red wine (in this case, pinot noir) during the disgorgement process. The richness of this Chandon rosé works well with the spicy avocado and the salty salmon roe.

Crunchy little pancakes with a lively topping, passed around as an appetiser with pre-dinner drinks, mean you don't need a first course. And the main course of chicken with great accompaniments is fast and fuss-free.

ROASTED CHICKEN WITH BRAISED LEEKS AND SOY AND OLIVE DRESSING

360g (2 cups) wild rice
30g butter
2 tablespoons pinenuts, roasted
1/4 cup chopped mixed herbs (including
    flat-leaf parsley, basil, coriander)
2 x 1.8kg free-range chickens,
    each jointed into 4 pieces
    (use carcases for chicken stock)
Olive oil
4 leeks, white part only,
    halved lengthwise and crosswise
1/3 cup chicken stock (see basic recipes)
6 baby bok choy, leaves separated

SOY AND OLIVE DRESSING

150g whole canned pimentos, drained
1 clove of garlic, crushed
1 1/2 tablespoons soy sauce
2 1/2 tablespoons rice-wine vinegar
2 1/2 tablespoons balsamic vinegar
4 green onions, finely chopped
1/3 cup peanut oil
1/3 cup extra virgin olive oil
90g (1/2 cup) small black olives

For soy and olive dressing, remove seeds from pimentos and cut into thin strips. Combine garlic, soy sauce, vinegars and green onion and whisk in combined oils. Stir in pimento and olives and check seasoning.

Cook wild rice in boiling, salted water for 30 minutes or until cooked. Drain, add butter, pinenuts and herbs and season to taste.

Meanwhile, brush chicken pieces with olive oil, brown all over in a hot frying pan, transfer to a roasting pan and roast at 200C for 15-20 minutes or until cooked. Rest in a warm place for 5 minutes.

Heat 2 tablespoons olive oil in a large heavy-based saucepan, add leek and stock and cook, covered, over low heat until leek is tender. Stir-fry bok choy in a little of the leek pan juices until just wilted, then season to taste.

Spoon wild-rice mixture onto 8 plates, top with braised leeks, bok choy and chicken and spoon dressing over.

wine: Frankland Estate Isolation Ridge Chardonnay, Frankland River, WA. This wine is refined and tightly structured with a lemony acidity that adds zest and drive to the finish.

GOAT'S CHEESE WITH APPLE WEDGES AND OAT BISCUITS

Chabichou du Poitou,
    or another firm, mature goat's cheese
Pink lady apple wedges
    and oat biscuits, to serve

Serve goat's cheese with apple wedges and oat biscuits.

wine: Mount Pleasant Rosehill Shiraz, Hunter Valley, NSW. Hunter Valley shiraz is typically softer, less oaky and shows more vinosity than the bold-fruited and more potent shiraz styles from South Australia. The Rosehill vineyard is more than 50 years old and it produces wines of great depth and character, without undue oak influence.

ROASTED CHICKEN WITH BRAISED LEEKS AND SOY AND OLIVE DRESSING

BITTER-CHOCOLATE TART

The pastry in this tart is very soft and can be quite difficult to roll, especially on a warm day. Alternatively, you can simply press the pastry into the tart tin.

175g soft unsalted butter, chopped
75g icing sugar
2 egg yolks
250g (1 2/3 cups) plain flour
Dutch cocoa, for dusting

FILLING

250g dark couverture chocolate
    (70% cocoa solids), chopped
165g unsalted butter, chopped
2 eggs
3 egg yolks
50g caster sugar

Combine butter and icing sugar in a food processor and process until light and creamy. Add egg yolks one at a time, processing well after each. Add 25ml cold water and process to combine. Transfer mixture to a large bowl, then fold in flour and form into a disc. Wrap in plastic wrap and refrigerate for 2 hours.

Roll out pastry on a lightly floured surface until 5mm thick and line a 28cm tart tin with removable base with pastry. Cover and freeze for 1 hour. Line pastry with baking paper, fill with dried beans or rice and bake at 200C for 10 minutes. Remove paper and beans and bake until base is golden. Cool.

For filling, melt chocolate and butter in the top of a double saucepan or in a heatproof bowl over simmering water. Whisk eggs, egg yolks and sugar until pale and creamy, then fold in the slightly cooled chocolate mixture. Pour mixture into prepared pastry shell and bake at 130C for 10 minutes. Custard should begin to set around edges but still be slightly wobbly in the centre. Cool, then serve dusted with cocoa.

wine: Penfolds Magill Bluestone Tawny. This Penfolds port has walnut, rancio characters underpinned by a rather floral spirit (similar to cognac) which is well met by the intensity of the chocolate.

other menu suggestions

warm weather

These menus were compiled by
Kathy Snowball from recipes in this book.
Some quantities may need to be adjusted.

menu serves 6

grilled pear, mozzarella and prosciutto salad (page 18)

baked lamb topside with roasted ratatouille and green sauce (page 78)
   and steamed kipfler potatoes

baked figs with raspberries (page 70) and mascarpone

menu serves 8

warm olives with eggplant dip (page 20) and toasted turkish bread

chicken-liver pâté with toasts and cornichons (page 42)

moreton bay bugs with pappardelle, saffron and tomato (page 69)

plum, walnut and pinenut tarts (page 78) with thick cream

menu serves 8

corn soup shots (page 24)

salsa agresto with penne, asparagus and butter beans (page 70)

leek and artichoke tart (page 66) with radicchio salad (page 23)

orange sorbet with honeydew melon (page 48)

menu serves 8

roasted-tomato gazpacho with basil oil (page 80)

cumin-roasted spatchcock with coriander and red-onion salad (page 30)
   and tabouli (page 28)

mango and strawberry meringue cake (page 28)

menu serves 8

char-grilled octopus with roasted-vegetable salad and hummus (page 45)

blue-eye kebabs with preserved-lemon and mint marinade (page 89)

spinach and herb risoni (page 62)

mixed-pea and bean salad (page 83)

pistachio spice cake with stone fruit in vanilla syrup (page 69)
   and crème anglaise (page 178)

menu serves 10

marinated leeks with prawns and feta (page 78)

barbecued whole rump with panzanella (page 46)
   and rocket and pumpkin salad (page 46)

vanilla-bean ice-cream sandwich with berries and red-wine syrup (page 84)

cool weather

These menus were compiled by
Kathy Snowball from recipes in this book.
Some quantities may need to be adjusted.

menu serves 6

antipasto of white-bean purée and salad, swiss-brown mushroom and shallot frittata,
   wilted salad with roasted hazelnuts and goat's cheese (pages 146 and 149)
spaghetti with peas and chicory (page 121)
vin santo zabaglione with strawberries and pinenut biscuits (page 101)

menu serves 6

crisp prosciutto and shaved-fennel salad (page 126) with sourdough
poached chicken with winter vegetables and tarragon pistou (page 149)
glazed vanilla quince and rhubarb with chocolate pots (page 114)

menu serves 8

salt-cod brandade (page 107) with Italian-style bread
lamb shanks with white beans and picada (page 113) and baby spinach salad
self-saucing chocolate and espresso pudding (page 144)
   with vanilla-bean ice-cream (page 84)

menu serves 4

crumbed eggplant with roasted tomatoes and basil (page 118)
seared salmon with rocket and prawn mash (page 162)
apple and ginger brioche pudding (page 116) with honey yoghurt

menu serves 6

carrot soup with dill (page 102)
pork cutlets with corn and sage pancakes (page 144) and wilted spinach
coffee and vanilla-bean crème caramel (page 129)

menu serves 8

warm avocado, grapefruit and scallop salad (page 144)
poached fillet of beef with grilled witlof and horseradish cream (page 152)
blood-orange and almond cake with rosewater cream (page 162)

basic recipe

CHICKEN STOCK

1 x 1.5kg free-range chicken
500g chicken wings
1 onion, chopped
1 large carrot, sliced
1 stick of celery, sliced
1 leek, white part only, sliced
6 sprigs of parsley
1 bay leaf
1 sprig of thyme

Combine chicken and wings with remaining ingredients in a stockpot and add enough cold water to cover by 2cm. Bring to a simmer and cook for 30 minutes, skimming scum from surface.

Reduce heat to a gentle simmer and cook for 1 hour. Remove whole chicken and reserve meat for salads and sandwiches. Return carcase to stockpot and continue cooking for another 3 hours, occasionally adding enough water to keep contents submerged.

Cool slightly, then strain stock through a sieve lined with damp muslin. Cool to room temperature, cover and refrigerate until cold, then remove fat from surface. Can be refrigerated for up to 3 days or frozen for up to 3 months.

Makes about 3 litres.

VEGETABLE STOCK

2 onions, quartered
4 tomatoes, halved
2 tablespoons olive oil
2 carrots, sliced
6 cloves of garlic, halved
1 leek, white part only, sliced
12 sprigs of parsley
3 sprigs of thyme
1 bay leaf
1/2 bunch spinach, trimmed
    and chopped (see note)
2cm strip of lemon peel, pith removed
100g button mushrooms, sliced
10 black peppercorns

Combine onion, tomato and half the oil in a roasting pan and roast at 220C for 30 minutes.

Meanwhile, heat remaining oil in a stockpot, add carrot, garlic and leek and cook over medium heat for 5 minutes or until vegetables are soft. Add remaining ingredients, roasted vegetables and enough water to cover by 2cm. Bring to a simmer and cook for 2 hours, skimming scum from surface.

Cool slightly, then strain stock through a sieve lined with damp muslin, pressing down on vegetables to extract all liquid. Cool to room temperature, then cover and refrigerate. Can be refrigerated for up to 4 days or frozen for up to 3 months.

Makes about 2.5 litres.

Note: Omit the spinach if a white stock is required, as spinach will give the stock a muddy green colour.

FISH STOCK

Flat fish are ideal for making stock due to their high gelatinous and low fat content. Cut vegetables finely so that their flavours can be easily extracted during the short cooking time. If stock is cloudy, set aside and, when solids have settled to the bottom, carefully ladle off clear liquid. This stock has a delicate flavour and is suitable for poaching. It can be reduced if a more concentrated flavour is desired.

2 tablespoons olive oil
Bones and heads of 6 flathead,
    rinsed well
250ml dry white wine
1 carrot, chopped
1/2 stick of celery, thinly sliced
1/2 leek, white part only, thinly sliced
4 sprigs of flat-leaf parsley
2 sprigs of lemon thyme
2 bay leaves
3 tomatoes, chopped

Heat oil in a stockpot, add fish carcases and cook, stirring occasionally, over medium heat for 5 minutes until flesh and bones are white. Add wine and stir to pick up any sediment. Add remaining ingredients and enough water to cover by 2cm. Bring to a simmer and cook for 20 minutes, skimming scum from surface. Stand for 15 minutes, then strain stock through a sieve lined with damp muslin, pressing down on solids to extract as much liquid as possible. Strain again through clean, damp muslin to remove all traces of solid matter. Cool, cover and refrigerate. Best used on the day it is made.

Makes about 2 litres.

VEAL STOCK

2kg veal shanks, cut into 5cm pieces
1kg veal shoulder, cut into 4cm pieces
Olive oil
2 onions, quartered
1 large head of garlic, halved crosswise
2 carrots, sliced
1 stick of celery, sliced
4 tomatoes, halved
200g button mushrooms, sliced
5g dried porcini mushrooms
6 sprigs of parsley
3 sprigs of thyme
2 bay leaves
10 black peppercorns

Place veal shanks and meat in 1 or 2 large flameproof dishes (do not overcrowd), drizzle with oil and toss to coat. Roast at 200C for 1 hour, turning over after 30 minutes. Add onion, garlic, carrot, celery and tomato, mix gently and cook for 45 minutes or until meat is well browned.

Using a slotted spoon, transfer mixture to a stockpot and add enough cold water to cover by 2cm. Bring to a simmer and cook for 30 minutes, skimming scum from surface.

Meanwhile, discard fat from cooking juices in baking dish, place dish over high heat and deglaze pan with 1 cup water, stirring to pick up any sediment. Add to stockpot with remaining ingredients and simmer gently for at least 4 hours or up to 8 hours for a more intense flavour, occasionally adding enough water to keep contents submerged.

Cool to room temperature, then strain stock through a sieve lined with damp muslin, pressing down on solids to extract all liquid. Cover and refrigerate until cold, then remove fat from surface. Can be refrigerated for up to 4 days or frozen for up to 3 months. For use in sauces, reduce stock to a sticky, thick glaze.

Makes about 2 litres.

basic recipes

QUICK MARINADE

2 tablespoons extra virgin olive oil
2 tablespoons balsamic vinegar
1 tablespoon seeded mustard
1 teaspoon hot english mustard
Beef or lamb, to serve

Combine all ingredients in a small bowl and whisk well.

Place beef or lamb in a shallow glass or ceramic dish and pour marinade over, turn meat to coat and stand at room temperature for 5 minutes. Char-grill or barbecue meat, brushing with any remaining marinade, until cooked to your liking.

Makes enough for 1kg rump or lamb chops, to serve 4.

KAFFIR-LIME LEAF MARINADE

6 kaffir-lime leaves, thinly sliced
1 fresh, small red chilli,
     seeded and chopped
4 green onions, chopped
2 cloves of garlic, chopped
2 tablespoons lime juice
1/2 teaspoon fish sauce
1/2 cup light olive oil
Fish or other seafood, to serve

Blend all ingredients in a blender until finely chopped.

Place fish fillets or other seafood, such as green prawns, in a shallow glass or ceramic dish. Pour marinade over and turn fish or prawns to coat, then cover and refrigerate for 1 hour. Drain fish or prawns, then barbecue or char-grill, turning once, until just cooked.

Makes enough for 4 fish fillets or 1kg green prawns, to serve 4.

MOROCCAN-SPICE MARINADE

2 teaspoons cumin seeds, roasted
2 teaspoons coriander seeds, roasted
1 cup coriander leaves
1 tablespoon grated ginger
2 teaspoons ground sweet paprika
2 teaspoons ground turmeric
2 cloves of garlic, chopped
2 teaspoons salt
1/4 cup lemon juice
1/4 cup olive oil
1/2 teaspoon Tabasco
Poultry or game, to serve

Process all ingredients in a food processor until well combined.

Place poultry or game pieces in a shallow glass or ceramic dish, pour marinade over and turn to coat. Cover and refrigerate for 8 hours. Drain poultry or game, reserving marinade.

Place poultry or game in a roasting pan fitted with a wire rack and roast at 200C until just tender, brushing with reserved marinade during cooking. Rest in a warm place for 5 minutes before serving.

Makes enough for 1 free-range chicken, quartered, or 4 butterflied spatchcocks, to serve 4.

POMEGRANATE-MOLASSES MARINADE

2 tablespoons pomegranate molasses
2 tablespoons lemon juice
2 cloves of garlic, finely chopped
1/2 teaspoon sugar
1/4 cup olive oil
1 tablespoon honey
1 teaspoon salt
Poultry or game, to serve

Combine all ingredients and whisk well.

Place poultry or game pieces in a shallow glass or ceramic dish, pour marinade over and turn to coat. Cover and refrigerate for 8 hours. Drain poultry or game, reserving marinade.

Barbecue or char-grill poultry or game over medium-high heat, brushing with reserved marinade, until just cooked.

Makes enough for 4 chicken breast fillets flattened to an even thickness or 4 large butterflied quail, to serve 4.

BASIC SALAD DRESSING

1 clove of garlic, halved
1/2 cup extra virgin olive oil
2 tablespoons lemon juice
     or balsamic vinegar

Rub bowl with garlic, then add oil, whisk in lemon juice or vinegar and season to taste with sea salt and cracked black pepper.

Makes 2/3 cup.

LEMON, CAPER AND OLIVE DRESSING

50g pitted green olives, chopped
25g pitted black olives, chopped
20g rinsed and drained capers, chopped
1 tablespoon chopped dill
2 green onions, finely chopped
2/3 cup basic salad dressing
     (see above), using lemon juice,
     not balsamic vinegar

Combine all ingredients and season to taste.

Makes 1 cup.

CURRANT AND PINENUT DRESSING

35g (1/4 cup) currants
50g (1/4 cup) roasted pinenuts
1/2 cup chopped flat-leaf parsley
2/3 cup basic salad dressing (see above)

Soak currants in boiling water for 5 minutes, then drain. Add currants, pinenuts and parsley to basic salad dressing and combine well. Season to taste.

Makes 1 cup.

BASIC MAYONNAISE

3 egg yolks
2 teaspoons dijon mustard
2 tablespoons lemon or lime juice
1 cup olive oil
2 tablespoons lemon or lime juice,
   extra, optional

Process egg yolks, mustard and juice in a food processor until well combined. With motor running, gradually add oil in a thin stream until mixture is thick and pale. Whisk in extra juice or cold water to reach the desired consistency. Season to taste.

   Makes 1 1/2 cups.

BASIL MAYONNAISE

Process egg yolks, dijon mustard and juice as for basic mayonnaise (see above) in a food processor until well combined, then add 1/2 cup firmly packed basil leaves and 2 cloves of garlic and process until smooth. With motor running, gradually add 1 cup olive oil in a thin stream until mixture is thick and pale. Whisk in 2 tablespoons extra lemon or lime juice or cold water to reach the desired consistency. Season to taste.

   Makes 1 1/2 cups.

WASABI MAYONNAISE

Process egg yolks, dijon mustard and juice as for basic mayonnaise (see above) in a food processor until well combined, then add 1 teaspoon wasabi powder and process until smooth. With motor running, gradually add 1 cup olive oil in a thin stream until mixture is thick and pale. Whisk in 2 tablespoons extra lemon or lime juice or cold water to reach the desired consistency. Season to taste.

   Makes 1 1/2 cups.

DILL AND MUSTARD MAYONNAISE

Combine 4 egg yolks, 2 teaspoons dijon mustard and 1/3 cup lemon juice in a food processor and process until well combined. While motor is running, add 1 1/4 cups olive oil in a thin, steady stream until thick. Add 1/3 cup chopped dill and a little milk if too thick and process until well combined and the consistency of thick cream. Season to taste.

   Makes about 2 cups.

BASIC PESTO

2 cups firmly packed basil leaves
60g parmesan, grated
40g (1/4 cup) pinenuts
1 clove of garlic, chopped
1/3 cup olive oil

Process basil, parmesan, pinenuts and garlic in a food processor until well combined. With motor running, gradually add oil in a thin stream and process until smooth. Season to taste.

   Makes 1 cup.

MINT PESTO

Process 1 cup firmly packed mint leaves and 1 cup firmly packed flat-leaf parsley leaves with parmesan, pinenuts and garlic as for basic pesto (see above) in a food processor until well combined. With motor running, gradually add oil in a thin stream and process until smooth. Season to taste.

   Makes 1 cup.

SPINACH AND WALNUT PESTO

Roast 100g (1/2 cup) walnut halves until lightly browned. Process walnuts and 55g (1 cup) trimmed, washed spinach leaves in a food processor until finely chopped. With motor running, gradually add 1/2 cup olive oil in a thin stream and process until smooth. Add 40g (1/2 cup) grated parmesan, season to taste and process until combined.

   Makes 1 1/4 cups.

SALSA VERDE

2 cups firmly packed mixed herbs
   (including flat-leaf parsley, basil,
   coriander, mint)
2 cloves of garlic, chopped
3 anchovy fillets, drained and chopped
2 teaspoons salt-packed capers,
   rinsed and drained
1/4 cup lemon juice
1/4 cup olive oil

Process herbs, garlic, anchovy, capers and lemon juice in a food processor until well combined. With motor running, gradually add oil in a thin stream and process until smooth. Season to taste.

   Makes 1 cup.

TARRAGON PISTOU

2 cloves of garlic, chopped
1 cup firmly packed tarragon leaves
   (about 2 large bunches)
50g parmesan, grated
1/3 cup extra virgin olive oil

Process all ingredients in a food processor until smooth. Season to taste.

   Makes about 2/3 cup.

HUMMUS

200g (1 cup) dried chickpeas,
   soaked in 3 cups cold water
   overnight, then drained
1 bay leaf
1 cinnamon stick
1/2 cup lemon juice
1/2 cup tahini
4 cloves of garlic, chopped
1/4 cup olive oil

Place chickpeas, bay leaf and cinnamon in a large saucepan with 2 litres cold water and bring to the boil. Simmer, uncovered, for 1 hour until chickpeas are very soft. Drain and reserve cooking liquid. Discard bay leaf and cinnamon stick.

   Process chickpeas, 1/4 cup reserved cooking liquid and remaining ingredients in a food processor until smooth. Season well with sea salt and freshly ground black pepper.

   Makes about 3 cups.

basic recipes

QUICK TOMATO SAUCE

1 x 400g can whole tomatoes, crushed
1 clove of garlic, chopped
2 tablespoons olive oil
1 tablespoon shredded basil leaves

Combine crushed tomatoes and their juice, garlic, oil and a pinch each of sugar and sea salt in a small saucepan. Cook over medium heat for about 10 minutes until thick. Add basil and season to taste.

Makes 1 cup.

ROASTED-TOMATO SAUCE WITH OLIVES AND CAPERS

1kg ripe egg tomatoes,
    halved lengthwise and seeded
1/4 cup olive oil
2 teaspoons dried oregano
1/2 teaspoon sugar
150ml verjuice
1 tablespoon tomato paste
80g (1/2 cup) kalamata olives,
    pitted and chopped
2 tablespoons rinsed
    and drained capers

Place tomato, cut side up, in a roasting pan. Drizzle with oil, sprinkle with oregano and sugar and season to taste. Roast at 180C for 30 minutes, then add combined verjuice and tomato paste and roast for another 15 minutes. Process half the tomato mixture in a food processor until smooth. Chop remaining tomato and stir into purée with remaining ingredients, then check seasoning and adjust if necessary.

Makes about 3 cups.

TOMATO FRUIT CHUTNEY

1kg tomatoes, chopped
1 large onion, chopped
80g sultanas
80g fresh ginger, peeled and chopped
Grated rind of 3 lemons
1 cinnamon stick
400g chopped apple and pear
400ml white-wine vinegar
400g sugar

Combine all ingredients in a heavy-based saucepan and simmer, uncovered, over low heat for 3-4 hours or until chutney is thick. Remove cinnamon stick, spoon chutney into sterilised jars and seal while hot. Store in a dark place and refrigerate after opening.

Makes about 4 cups.

TAPENADE

350g black or green olives,
    pitted and chopped
2 cloves of garlic, chopped
5 anchovy fillets, drained and chopped
2 tablespoons rinsed and drained capers
100ml olive oil

Process all ingredients, except oil, in a food processor until well combined. With motor running, add oil in a thin stream to form a thick paste, then check seasoning and adjust if necessary.

Makes about 1 1/3 cups.

PEELED CAPSICUM

Place whole capsicum over a gas flame or on a barbecue and turn over heat until skin has blackened and blistered. Alternatively, halve capsicum lengthwise, place skin side up on an oven tray and grill until skin is blackened and blistered. Place capsicum in a paper bag and seal for 15 minutes before removing skin.

ROASTED CAPSICUM

2 red capsicum, sliced
2 tablespoons olive oil
2 teaspoons brown sugar
1 tablespoon balsamic vinegar
2 tablespoons baby basil leaves

Place capsicum in a roasting pan, drizzle with oil, sprinkle with sugar, season to taste and roast at 200C for 20 minutes or until browned and tender.

Serve warm or at room temperature drizzled with vinegar and sprinkled with basil.

Other vegetables, such as zucchini, eggplant and spanish onion, can be roasted in the same way.

TAMARIND PASTE

Tamarind is the soft, dried pulp of the tamarind pod. To make tamarind paste or liquid, place tamarind in a bowl, cover with hot water and stand until cool. Work the tamarind with your fingers to release as much pulp as possible, then strain and use as directed. Using only a small amount of water will give a paste; adding more water will produce tamarind liquid. Tamarind paste is also available in jars from Asian food stores.

BASIC RISOTTO

2 tablespoons olive oil
1 onion, chopped
1 clove of garlic, chopped
300g (1½ cups) arborio rice
100ml dry white wine
1 litre chicken stock
    (see basic recipes), approximately
100g grated parmesan
20g butter

Heat oil in a large saucepan and cook onion over low heat until soft. Add garlic and rice and stir over low heat until coated with oil and lightly roasted. Add wine and stir over medium heat until absorbed. Have stock simmering in another saucepan. Add 1 cup stock to rice mixture and stir over low-medium heat until stock is absorbed. Add remaining stock, ½ cup at a time, stirring constantly, allowing each addition to be absorbed before adding the next. Add parmesan and butter with the last addition of stock, then season to taste. Turn off heat and stand, covered, for 5 minutes before serving.

Serves 4.

HERB RISOTTO

With the last addition of stock (see basic risotto, above), add ½ cup chopped flat-leaf parsley or basil or a combination of both and 1 tablespoon grated lemon rind with the parmesan and butter.

LEEK, BLUE CHEESE AND SWEET-POTATO RISOTTO

Heat 2 tablespoons oil in a large saucepan and cook 2 chopped leeks over low heat until soft. Proceed as for basic risotto (see above) until the last addition of stock. At this stage, add 500g peeled, chopped and roasted sweet potato, 1 tablespoon chopped chives and 100g crumbled blue cheese with stock, then season to taste. Turn off heat and stand, covered, for 5 minutes before serving.

SOFT POLENTA

2 litres milk
1 onion, quartered
4 sprigs of thyme
2 bay leaves
1 teaspoon salt
150g polenta

Combine milk, onion, thyme and bay leaves in a heavy-based saucepan and slowly bring to the boil. Remove from heat and stand for 15 minutes for flavours to infuse. Strain, return milk to a clean saucepan, bring to the boil, add salt and slowly whisk in polenta. Cook polenta over lowest heat, stirring regularly with a whisk, for about 30 minutes or until soft. Season to taste. The polenta should be soft and flowing. If it is too stiff, add some boiling water.

Serves 6-8.

SHORTCRUST PASTRY

250g (1²/₃ cups) plain flour
125g cold butter, chopped

Combine flour and a pinch of salt in a food processor. Add butter and ⅓ cup cold water and process for 20 seconds until mixture just comes together. Knead dough gently to form a disc, cover with plastic wrap and refrigerate for 30 minutes.

Roll out dough on a lightly floured surface until large enough to line a 23cm tart tin with removable base. Cover and refrigerate for 30 minutes.

Line pastry with baking paper, fill with dried beans or rice and bake at 180C for 12-15 minutes. Remove paper and beans and bake for another 5-8 minutes or until pastry is dry and crisp.

This tart shell is suitable for both sweet and savoury fillings.

SWEET SHORTCRUST PASTRY

100g cold unsalted butter, chopped
250g (1²/₃ cups) plain flour
100g icing sugar
2 x 60g eggs
1 tablespoon grated lemon rind

Process butter, sifted flour, icing sugar and a pinch of salt in a food processor until mixture resembles breadcrumbs. Add eggs and lemon rind and process until mixture just comes together. Knead dough gently to form a disc, cover with plastic wrap and refrigerate for 30 minutes.

Roll out dough on a lightly floured surface until large enough to line a 23cm tart tin with removable base. Cover and refrigerate for 30 minutes.

Line pastry with baking paper, fill with dried beans or rice and bake at 180C for 12-15 minutes. Remove paper and beans and bake for another 5-8 minutes or until pastry is dry and crisp.

basic recipes

QUICK PUFF PASTRY

200g (1 1/3 cups) plain flour
200g cold butter, chopped

Combine flour, butter and 1/2 teaspoon salt in a food processor and, using the pulse button, process until mixture resembles coarse breadcrumbs. Add 1/4 cup cold water and process until mixture just comes together. The dough will be crumbly at this stage. Turn dough onto a clean surface and, using the heel of your hand, push dough away from you in sections to smear the butter. Form pastry into a rectangle, cover with plastic wrap and refrigerate for 10 minutes. Roll out pastry on a lightly floured surface to form a 18x40cm rectangle. Fold bottom third of pastry up over the centre and then fold the top third down to cover it. Cover with plastic wrap and refrigerate for 20 minutes. Place chilled pastry on lightly floured surface and give it a quarter turn anti-clockwise. The top flap should be to your left. Roll out dough as before to form a 18x40cm rectangle. Repeat folding and turning dough a quarter anti-clockwise. Repeat once more, then fold as before, cover and refrigerate for at least 30 minutes before using.

Pastry will keep, covered, in the refrigerator for 1 day or frozen for 1 month.

Makes about 500g of pastry.

CREME ANGLAISE

3 egg yolks
55g (1/4 cup) caster sugar
300ml milk
1 vanilla bean, split lengthwise

Whisk egg yolks and sugar in a bowl until well combined and sugar is dissolved. Combine milk, scraped seeds of vanilla bean and bean in a saucepan, bring just to the boil, then remove from heat. Gradually whisk hot milk mixture into egg mixture until combined. Transfer mixture to the top of a double saucepan or a heatproof bowl over a pan of simmering water and stir constantly until mixture thickens enough to coat the back of a wooden spoon. Do not boil. Serve warm or at room temperature with desserts.

Makes about 1 1/4 cups.

CARDAMOM SYRUP

3 cardamom pods, crushed
1 vanilla bean, split lengthwise
110g (1/2 cup) caster sugar
2 teaspoons lemon or lime juice
Mixed berries and peaches, to serve

Combine cardamom, scraped seeds of vanilla bean, vanilla bean, sugar and 1 1/2 cups water in a saucepan and stir over medium heat until sugar dissolves, then bring to the boil. Reduce heat and simmer for 10 minutes. Cool. Combine syrup and citrus juice in a bowl and refrigerate for at least 1 hour or up to 8 hours for flavours to develop.

Serve syrup with mixed berries and peaches. Makes about 2 cups.

CARAMEL, RUM AND RAISIN SYRUP

110g (1/2 cup) caster sugar
1/2 cup light corn syrup
100ml rum
85g (1/2 cup) raisins
Pancakes and vanilla ice-cream,
  to serve

Combine sugar and corn syrup in a saucepan and stir over low heat until sugar dissolves. Increase heat and boil until golden, brushing down side of pan with water. Remove from heat, carefully add 1/2 cup water and rum and stir over low heat until smooth. Add raisins and simmer for 5-10 minutes or until syrup begins to thicken. Serve syrup warm or at room temperature over pancakes with vanilla ice-cream.

Makes about 1 1/2 cups.

SPICED WHITE-WINE SUGAR SYRUP

250ml fruity white wine, such as riesling
330g (1 1/2 cups) caster sugar
1 cinnamon stick
6 white peppercorns
4 cloves
3 cardamom pods
Peel of 1/2 lemon
Poached pears and apples
  or mixed melon salad, to serve

Combine wine, 1 cup water, sugar, cinnamon stick, peppercorns, cloves, cardamom and lemon peel in a saucepan and stir over low heat until sugar dissolves. Bring to the boil and simmer over medium heat until reduced and syrupy. Poach pears and apples in unstrained syrup, or cool to room temperature, strain, then cover and refrigerate. Pour strained cold syrup over mixed melon salad.

Makes about 2 cups.

BLACKBERRY SYRUP

400g blackberries
75g (1/3 cup) sugar
Crêpes or waffles, to serve

Combine blackberries with sugar and 1/2 cup water in a saucepan, bring to the boil and simmer, stirring occasionally, for 10 minutes or until fruit is soft. Push mixture through a sieve. Return syrup to pan and simmer for another 5-10 minutes or until thick. Cool to room temperature, then cover and refrigerate. Serve over crêpes or waffles or use as a cocktail base.

Makes about 1 1/2 cups.

glossary

ACIDULATED WATER: water with lemon juice added, to prevent discolouration of vegetables and fruits once they have been peeled.

AGED BALSAMIC VINEGAR: concentrated, complex balsamic vinegar from Modena in Italy, bearing the words, *aceto balsimico tradizionale di Modena*.

AL DENTE: until just cooked. Refers mainly to pasta, rice and vegetables.

BAKE BLIND: to bake a pastry case lined with baking paper and filled with rice or dried beans to prevent sides from collapsing during cooking.

BAKING PAPER: also known as parchment or non-stick baking paper. Used to line pans.

BAKING POWDER: a raising agent consisting mainly of two parts cream of tartar to one part bicarbonate of soda (baking soda).

BARBECUED CHINESE DUCK: available from Chinese barbecue shops.

BASTE: to spoon fat, wine or stock over food during cooking, to add flavour and prevent food from drying out.

BEETROOT: also known as beets or red beets. Firm, round root vegetables with edible leaves. Can be eaten raw, boiled or roasted.

BLACK FUNGUS: sometimes called wood-ear or cloud-ear mushroom because of its wrinkly appearance. Available from Asian food stores and some greengrocers.

BLACK ONION SEEDS: sometimes called nigella or kalonji. Seeds have a peppery taste and are used in Indian and Middle Eastern cooking. Available from spice stores and Middle Eastern food stores.

BLANCH: to cook briefly in boiling, salted water, then drain and refresh under cold water.

BISCUITS: also known as cookies.

BOUQUET GARNI: flavouring for soups and stews made from bay leaf and sprigs of parsley, thyme and marjoram tied together with string.

BRESAOLA: cured dried beef fillet, served in thin slices as an entrée or as part of an antipasto plate.

BROAD BEANS: also known as fava beans. Available fresh or frozen.

BUCKWHEAT: a grain that may be roasted and used whole or made into flour and used in the same way as other cereal grains. It has a pleasant nutty flavour.

BUFFALO MOZZARELLA: Italian-style mozzarella made from buffalo milk. Available from delicatessens and cheese shops.

BURGHUL: hulled wheat that has been steamed until partly cooked, then dried and cracked or crushed into coarse or fine grains. Available from some supermarkets, delicatessens and Middle Eastern food stores.

BUTTER: use salted or unsalted (sweet) butter as directed (125g is equal to one stick of butter).

BUTTER BEANS: yellow, waxy fresh beans, a variety of the green bean.

BUTTERMILK: sold alongside other milk products in supermarkets. Low in fat (1.8g fat per 100ml), it is good for desserts, baking and salad dressings.

CANNELLINI BEANS: small, dried white beans.

CAPSICUM: also known as pepper or bell pepper. Discard seeds and membrane before use. Banana capsicum are long, thin and mild in flavour and are used as a stuffed vegetable and in salads.

CASTER SUGAR: also known as superfine or finely granulated table sugar.

CHAT POTATO: baby new potato.

CORIANDER: also known as cilantro.

CORNICHON: small French gherkin.

COUVERTURE CHOCOLATE: top-quality bittersweet chocolate with a high percentage of cocoa butter and cocoa liquor. Available from good delicatessens and providores.

CUCUMBER: the telegraph cucumber is long with a coarse green skin, while the lebanese cucumber is about half the length and has a thinner skin.

DAIKON: long, white, smooth-skinned radish, used mostly in Asian recipes.

DARK SOY SAUCE: a dark, rich sauce that has fermented longer than light soy sauce. Used for colour and flavour.

DEGLAZE: to add liquid (water, wine, stock, verjuice) to the sediment and juices at the bottom of a pan – usually after frying meat, chicken or fish – and boil, stirring in the coagulated juices.

DEGORGE: to extract bitter juices from vegetables (eggplant, zucchini) by salting, then rinsing.

DRIED ROSE PETALS: available from Middle Eastern food stores.

EGGPLANT: also known as aubergine. Japanese and lebanese eggplants are varieties of baby eggplant.

FARRO: the oldest known wheat, dating back to the Pharaohs. Farro puls polenta is farro that has been milled to produce a coarse meal. It is used as a thickening agent and for flavour. Available from good delicatessens and providores.

FRENCHED: bone ends cleaned of meat.

GARAM MASALA: a blend of spices originating in North India and based on varying proportions of cardamom, cinnamon, cloves, coriander, fennel and cumin, roasted and ground together.

GELATINE LEAVES: transparent sheets with a faint crosshatched texture; 14g gelatine leaves will set 500ml (2 cups) of liquid (firm set) and is equivalent to 14g (1 tablespoon) powdered gelatine. Soak sheets in cold water for 5 minutes, squeeze out excess water, then add sheets to hot liquid.

GHEE: clarified butter with milk solids removed. It can be heated to a high temperature without burning.

GINGER JUICE: to make, finely grate a piece of ginger, place in a muslin or cloth and squeeze juice into a small bowl.

GOW GEE WRAPPERS: made from wheat flour and water. Available from some supermarkets and Asian food stores.

GREEN MUNG-BEAN NOODLES: shiny, thin, translucent noodles made from green mung beans; also known as cellophane noodles. Available from supermarkets and Asian food stores.

GREEN ONION: sometimes called shallot or scallion, it is an immature onion pulled when the top is still green and before the bulb has formed. Sold by the bunch.

GREEN PAWPAW: also known as green papaya. When in season, unripe pawpaw is available from most greengrocers. Green mango makes a good substitute.

GRENADINE: sweet, tart, red fruit syrup made from pomegranate juice. Used for colour and flavour.

HALOUMI: a firm, chewy cooked sheep's-milk cheese (it can also be made from cow's milk) that originated in Cyprus. Normally matured in brine and tasting a little like feta, it should be fried or grilled, then served immediately before it becomes rubbery. Available from some supermarkets and delicatessens.

HARISSA: fiery paste from North Africa, usually made from fresh or dried red chillies, garlic, dried coriander and mint, caraway seeds, fresh coriander, salt and olive oil. Available from some supermarkets, delicatessens and Middle Eastern food stores.

HONEY VINEGAR: Italian vinegar made from fermented diluted Piedmont honey. Good white-wine vinegar with a dash of honey to taste can be substituted.

ICING SUGAR: also known as powdered sugar or confectioner's sugar.

INFUSE: to heat gently, then stand to extract flavours from ingredients, as when infusing milk with a vanilla pod.

JULIENNE: to finely shred vegetables or citrus rind.

JUS: cooking juices or light stock served as a sauce.

KASSERI: a hard, mild white sheep's-milk cheese similar to provolone. Available from delicatessens and cheese shops.

KECAP MANIS: Indonesian sweet soy sauce. Available from some supermarkets and Asian food stores.

KEFALOTIRI (kefalotyri): a Greek sheep's-milk cheese, available from some supermarkets, good delicatessens and cheese shops.

KORMA CURRY PASTE: available from supermarkets and Asian food stores.

LEMON-PRESSED OLIVE OIL: an Italian olive oil, produced by crushing olives with lemons, then pressing the resulting pulp to produce an oil that captures the essence of the lemon as well as the olive. Extra virgin olive oil with grated lemon rind to taste can be substituted.

LIGHT SOY SAUCE: saltier and lighter in colour than dark soy sauce.

MACERATE: to soak food, usually fruit, in a liquid (wine, liqueur, juice) for flavours to develop.

MANDOLIN: slicer and shredder, used for vegetables.

MASCARPONE: a fresh, unripened cream cheese resembling thick clotted cream, with a slightly acidic, rich, sweet taste. Available from supermarkets.

MESCLUN: a salad mix of assorted young lettuce and other leaves, such as baby spinach, mizuna and curly endive.

MINCE MEAT: ground meat.

MIRIN: sweet rice wine, used only in cooking. Available from Asian food stores. Sweet sherry can be substituted.

MORETON BAY BUG: a member of the crustacean group of shellfish, it has white flesh and a rich sea taste. Crayfish, scampi or prawns can be substituted.

NORI SHEETS: shiny green sheets of dried seaweed, used to wrap around rice to make sushi. Available from delicatessens and Asian food stores.

OUZO: an aniseed-flavoured liqueur, also useful as a culinary flavouring.

PANKO: large Japanese breadcrumbs, available from Asian food stores. Day-old breadcrumbs can be substituted.

PAPPARDELLE: wide strips of pasta, sometimes with a crimped edge.

PARMIGIANO REGGIANO: parmesan cheese made by traditional methods within a defined area in Italy and aged for at least 18 months.

PAWPAW: also called papaya.

PEPITAS: dried pumpkin seeds.

PICADA: a traditional Spanish mixture of bread that is fried in olive oil, then mixed with nuts, herbs and garlic.

PIMENTO (canned): peeled and roasted sweet capsicum.

PIN-BONE: to remove small bones from fillets of fish, using tweezers.

PISTOU: a Provençal sauce, traditionally made from basil crushed with garlic and olive oil.

POLENTA: yellow-white coarse granular meal made from maize or corn. Also known as cornmeal.

POMEGRANATE MOLASSES: made from the juice of sour pomegranate seeds, boiled down to a thick syrup and used in salad dressings, casseroles, dips and desserts. Available from delicatessens and Middle Eastern food stores.

POMODORO: a thick, Italian-style tomato sauce. Available from supermarkets and delicatessens.

PONZU: a lemon-flavoured soy sauce, used in Japanese cooking. Available from Asian food stores.

PORCINI: dried Italian mushroom, also known as cep or boletus mushroom. Available from delicatessens. To use, soak in hot water for 15 minutes, drain, then chop, reserving liquid for stocks or casseroles.

POURING CREAM: also known as fresh or pure cream. It contains no additives and has a fat content of 35 per cent.

PRESERVED LEMON: lemons preserved in salt and lemon juice. A North African specialty.

PURE ORANGE OIL: a powerfully flavoured oil obtained from crushing and pressing oranges.

PUY LENTILS: very fine, dark blue-green lentils originally from Le Puy, France. Available from good delicatessens.

QUEENSLAND BLUE PUMPKIN: a medium-sized pumpkin with blossom and stem ends flattened. It has a deeply ribbed, hard slate-grey skin and bright orange flesh.

RAS EL HANOUT: Ground spice mix from North Africa with about 12 spices, including cinnamon, whole nutmeg, dried rosebuds, dried ginger, cloves and dried chilli. Available from spice stores and Middle Eastern food stores.

REFRESH: to rinse vegetables under cold water to halt the cooking process and to prevent loss of colour.

REST: **For pastry:** to set aside in a cool place to allow the gluten to relax, preventing tough pastry that will shrink. **For batter:** to set aside to allow starch to swell for a lighter result. **For meat, fish, poultry:** to set aside in a warm place to allow juices to set before serving (about 10-15 minutes for a whole roasted chicken or leg of lamb).

RICE-PAPER ROUNDS: translucent soluble sheets made from rice flour, water and salt. There is no substitute.

RISONI: a rice-shaped pasta available from supermarkets. Also known as orzo.

SAFFRON THREADS: threads from the dried stigmas of the crocus flower. Available from good food stores and some supermarkets.

SAKE: fermented rice wine, the national drink in Japan and also used in cooking. Available from liquor stores.

SAMBAL ULEK (sambal oelek): Indonesian chilli paste made from pounded chillies, salt, vinegar or tamarind. Available from supermarkets and Asian food stores.

SCAMPI: marine prawns with long, thin claws found in the deep waters of the Atlantic coast from Scandinavia to North Africa, and in north-western Australia.

SEASONED RICE WINE VINEGAR: available from Asian food stores.

SHALLOTS: also known as eschalots or french shallots. Small, teardrop-shaped, golden brown bulbs that are grown in clusters and sold by weight.

SHAOHSING RICE WINE: China's most famous rice wine, aged for at least 10 years to give it a warm amber colour. Used only in cooking. Available from Asian food stores.

SKORDALIA (skorthalia): a Greek sauce or accompaniment usually containing garlic, mashed potato or ground almonds, bread, olive oil and lemon juice.

SMOKY PAPRIKA: a Spanish-style paprika available in three different styles – sweet, bitter and hot. Choose according to taste.

SPANISH ONION: a large, purplish-red onion with a mild flavour. Also known as red onion.

SPINACH: english spinach.

SUMAC: ground spice from a slightly astringent, lemon-flavoured red berry. Available from Middle Eastern food stores and spice shops.

SWEETENED DRIED CRANBERRIES: available from supermarkets.

SWEET POTATO: a starchy root vegetable, also known as yam or kumara.

TAHINI: sesame-seed paste.

TAMARIND: soft dried pulp of the tamarind pod. To make tamarind paste or liquid, see page 176 in basic recipes.

VALPOLICELLA: a light red wine from north-eastern Italy.

VANILLA-BEAN HONEY: honey infused with a vanilla bean. Available from delicatessens. If not available, use ordinary honey.

VERJUICE: the unfermented juice of grapes, with a delicate lemon-vinegar flavour. Available from delicatessens.

ZA'ATAR: a Middle Eastern spice mixture, comprising equal quantities of sesame seeds, thyme and sumac with a little salt. Available from spice stores and Middle Eastern food stores.

ZEST: the very finely peeled rind of citrus fruit. Use a zester or peel rind very thinly, remove any white pith, then julienne.

ZUCCHINI: also known as courgette.

acknowledgments

Compiling an *Australian Gourmet Traveller* cookbook has been a joy for me, with so many fabulous recipes and photographs to choose from. The most difficult part was making the final choices, but I think you will find an excellent cross-section of your favourite recipes, plus many new ones, and something for almost every occasion. There are many people to thank on a project like this, but the silent heroes are the whole team at *Gourmet*, a dedicated bunch who constantly strive to produce the best magazine. Then there are our wonderful food writers, stylists and photographers, and I want to thank them for the high standard of their work and their attention to detail. I know that each contributor to the pages of *Gourmet* has a great love of food – and it shows. Special thanks to Bronwen Clark and Sophia Young for their outstanding recipes and styling and for their enthusiasm and energy, to Hieu Nguyen who has brought the book to life with his gorgeous design, and to Anna Macdonald for her vigilance and constant support. Thanks also to Peter Bourne for his excellent wine notes and to Meg Thomason for her charming introductions – both are invaluable additions to the book. Carolyn Lockhart, the former editor of *Australian Gourmet Traveller*, was a great source of inspiration for the book and was responsible over the years for shaping *Gourmet* and making it the most beautiful and prestigious food and travel magazine in Australia. My thanks also to current editor, Judy Sarris, who is passionate about the magazine and continues to drive it to new heights. This book is dedicated to you, our readers, who have given us so much support and encouragement – may you have many happy moments cooking from these recipes.

Kathy Snowball, Editor

RECIPES AND STYLING

Bronwen Clark: cocktail party, p32; smart dinner party, p38; christmas celebration, p50; classic dinner party, p92; simple asian lunch, p116; light asian dinner, p130; vegetarian indian banquet, p136; vegetarian dinner party, p154.

Jane Hann: informal dinner party, p146.

Suzie Smith: casual bistro lunch, p104.

Sophia Young: asian picnic, p10; vegetarian lunch party, p20; light birthday lunch, p24; cocktail party, p32; greek buffet, p58; lunch for friends, p66; summer brunch, p72; lazy summer picnic, p86; cosy sunday lunch, p110.

ADDITIONAL RECIPES

Allan Campion: baked lamb topside with roasted ratatouille and green sauce, p78.

Bronwen Clark: chicken-liver pâté with toasts and cornichons, p42; spiced calamari on lime-carrot salad, p56; thai-style red beef curry, p56; poached honey pears with ricotta, p102; braised pork neck with garlic and chilli paste, p121; coffee and vanilla-bean crème caramel, p129; self-saucing chocolate and espresso pudding, p144; crème anglaise, p178; cardamom syrup, p178; caramel, rum and raisin syrup, p178; spiced white-wine sugar syrup, p178; blackberry syrup, p178.

Fiona Hammond: carrot soup with dill, p102; vegetable stock, p173; fish stock, p173; veal stock, p173; quick puff pastry, p178.

Jane Hann: barbecued haloumi and asparagus with lemon salsa verde, p45; mascarpone mousse with bananas and peanut brittle, p56; marinated leeks with prawns and feta, p78; roasted-tomato gazpacho with basil oil, p80; poached whole ocean trout, p83; crisp prosciutto and shaved-fennel salad, p126; quick marinade, p174; kaffir-lime leaf marinade, p174; moroccan-spice marinade, p174; pomegranate-molasses marinade, p174; lemon, caper and olive dressing, p174; currant and pinenut dressing, p174; tarragon pistou, p175; roasted-tomato sauce with olives and capers, p176.

Lynne Mullins: italian dinner party, p98; crumbed eggplant with roasted tomatoes and basil, p118.

Louise Pickford: summer compote of watermelon and blackberries, p18; blood-orange and almond cake with rosewater cream, p162.

Damien Pignolet: winter fruit salad with buttermilk pudding, p122.

Kathy Snowball: grilled pear, mozzarella and prosciutto salad, p18; poached snapper with shaved asparagus and tomato and fennel-seed salad, p18; simple outdoor lunch, p30; char-grilled octopus with roasted-vegetable salad and hummus, p45; barbecued whole rump with panzanella, p46; rocket and pumpkin salad, p46; simple light dinner, p48; baked figs with raspberries, p70; vanilla-bean ice-cream sandwich with berries and red-wine syrup, p84; mushroom and buckwheat risotto with coriander pesto, p102; spaghetti with peas and chicory, p121; simple light dinner, p124; pan-fried tuna with spinach gnocchi and tomato and rosemary sauce, p129; poached fillet of beef with grilled witlof and horseradish cream, p152; rhubarb and strawberry compote with shortbread, p152; bresaola and shaved fennel with croûtons, p162; seared salmon with rocket and prawn mash, p162; elegant dinner party, p164; chicken stock, 173; basic salad dressing, p174; basic mayonnaise, p175; basic pesto, p175; salsa verde, p175; hummus, p175; dill and mustard mayonnaise, 175; quick tomato sauce, p176; tomato fruit chutney, p176; tapenade, p176; roasted and peeled capsicum, p176; tamarind paste, 176; basic risotto, p177; soft polenta, p177; shortcrust pastry, 177.

Sophia Young: macadamia, coconut and star-anise praline with tropical fruits, p46; bruschetta with pumpkin, gorgonzola and sage, p70; salsa agresto with penne, asparagus and butter beans, p70; plum, walnut and pinenut tarts, p78; warm avocado, grapefruit and scallop salad, p144; pork cutlets with corn and sage pancakes, p144; blue-cheese gougère, p152.

ADDITIONAL STYLING

Kristen Anderson: simple outdoor lunch, p30.
Ruth Armstrong: simple light lunch, p18; simple light dinner, p48; simple vegetarian lunch, p70; simple dinner party, p78; formal lunch, p80; simple vegetarian lunch, p102; simple light dinner, p124; simple sunday dinner, p144; simple dinner party, p152; simple celebration dinner, p162.
Bronwen Clark: warming winter lunch, p118.
Marie-Hélène Clauzon: italian dinner party, p98.
Jane Hann: sunday barbecue lunch, p42; simple asian dinner, p56; mediterranean dinner, p126; elegant dinner party, p164.
Sophia Young: cover; title page; contents page; foreword; section openers; other menus; acknowledgments page; basic recipes; glossary; index.
Food assistants: Rodney Dunn, Anna Beaumont and Chris Sheppard.

PHOTOGRAPHY

Quentin Bacon: casual bistro lunch, p104.
Alan Benson: foreword; sunday barbecue lunch, p42; greek buffet, p58; summer brunch, p72; cosy sunday lunch, p110; simple asian lunch, p116; warming winter lunch, p118; mediterranean dinner, p126; informal dinner party, p146.
Chris Chen: cocktail party, p32.
Georgie Cole: simple outdoor lunch, p30; smart dinner party, p38; christmas celebration, p50.
Rowan Fotheringham: simple asian dinner, p56.
Simon Griffiths: simple light lunch, p18; simple light dinner, p48; simple vegetarian lunch, p70; simple dinner party, p78; formal lunch, p80; simple vegetarian lunch, p102; simple light dinner, p124; simple sunday dinner, p144; simple dinner party, p152; simple celebration dinner, p162.
Louise Lister: title page; section openers; other menus; basic recipes; acknowledgments page; glossary; index; classic dinner party, p92; italian dinner party, p98; light asian dinner, p130; vegetarian indian banquet, p136; vegetarian dinner party, p154; elegant dinner party, p164.
Ashley Mackevicius: lunch for friends, p66.
George Seper: contents page; asian picnic, p10; vegetarian lunch party, p20; light birthday lunch, p24; lazy summer picnic, p86.
Ian Wallace: cover.

THANKS TO THESE STOCKISTS AND SUPPLIERS

Acorn Trading phone (02) 9518 9925
Alfresco Dining phone (02) 9958 7922
The Bay Tree phone (02) 9328 1101
Bison@Summers phone (02) 8308 0343
Country Road Homewear phone 1800 801 911
Demcos Seafoods phone (02) 9700 9000
Durina phone (02) 9874 9694
Empire Homewares phone (02) 9380 8877
Gaya Interiors phone (02) 9958 7033
Herbie's Spices phone (02) 9555 6035
Husk phone (03) 9827 2700
Malcolm Greenwood phone (02) 9953 8613
Market Import phone (03) 9500 0764
Minimax phone (03) 9826 0022
Mud Australia phone (02) 9518 0220
Orrefors/Kosta Boda phone (02) 9913 4200 or 1800 269 911
Orson & Blake phone (02) 9326 1155
Papaya phone (02) 9327 8411
The Parterre Garden phone (02) 9363 5874
Porter's Paints phone 1800 656 664
Rapee phone (02) 9496 4511
Ruby Star Traders phone (02) 9518 7899
Scullerymade phone (03) 9509 4003
Shack phone (02) 9884 7332
Supply & Demand phone (03) 9428 6912
Villeroy & Boch phone (02) 9975 3099 or 1800 252 770
Waterford Wedgwood phone 1300 852 022
Wheel & Barrow phone (02) 9878 5911

index

conversion chart

Wherever you live, you'll be able to use our recipes with the help of these conversions. While these conversions are only approximate, the difference between an exact and an approximate conversion of various liquid and dry measures is minimal and will not affect your cooking results.

measures

One Australian metric measuring cup holds approximately 250ml, one Australian metric tablespoon holds 20ml, one Australian metric teaspoon holds 5ml. The difference between one country's measuring cups and another's is within a two- or three-teaspoon variance. North America, New Zealand and the United Kingdom use a 15ml tablespoon.

All cup and spoon measurements are level.

We use large eggs with an average weight of 60g.

Unless specified, all fruit and vegetables are medium sized and herbs are fresh.

dry measures

metric	imperial
15g	1/2oz
30g	1oz
60g	2oz
90g	3oz
125g	4oz (1/4lb)
155g	5oz
185g	6oz
220g	7oz
250g	8oz (1/2lb)
280g	9oz
315g	10oz
345g	11oz
375g	12oz (3/4lb)
410g	13oz
440g	14oz
470g	15oz
500g	16oz (1lb)
750g	24oz (1 1/2lb)
1kg	32oz (2lb)

liquid measures

metric	imperial
30ml	1 fluid oz
60ml	2 fluid oz
100ml	3 fluid oz
125ml	4 fluid oz
150ml	5 fluid oz (1/4 pint/1 gill)
190ml	6 fluid oz
250ml	8 fluid oz
300ml	10 fluid oz (1/2 pint)
500ml	16 fluid oz
600ml	20 fluid oz (1 pint)
1000ml (1 litre)	1 3/4 pints

length measures

metric	imperial
3mm	1/8in
6mm	1/4in
1cm	1/2in
2cm	3/4in
2.5cm	1in
5cm	2in
6cm	2 1/2in
8cm	3in
10cm	4in
13cm	5in
15cm	6in
18cm	7in
20cm	8in
23cm	9in
25cm	10in
28cm	11in
30cm	12in (1ft)

OVEN TEMPERATURES

These oven temperatures are only a guide. Always check the manufacturer's manual.

	°C (Celsius)	°F (Fahrenheit)	Gas Mark
Very slow	120	250	1
Slow	150	300	2
Moderately slow	160	325	3
Moderate	180-190	350-375	4
Moderately hot	200-210	400-425	5
Hot	220-230	450-475	6
Very hot	240-250	500-525	7